# THE MACINTOSH
# SYSTEM FITNESS PLAN

# THE MACINTOSH SYSTEM FITNESS PLAN

## EASY EXERCISES TO IMPROVE PERFORMANCE AND RECLAIM DISK SPACE

Dan Shafer

**Addison-Wesley Publishing Company**

Reading, Massachusetts • Menlo Park, California • New York
Don Mills, Ontario • Wokingham, England • Amsterdam
Bonn • Sydney • Singapore • Tokyo • Madrid • San Juan
Paris • Seoul • Milan • Mexico City • Taipei

*Library of Congress Cataloging-in-Publication Data*

Shafer, Dan.
   The Macintosh system fitness plan  :  easy exercises to improve
performance and reclaim disk space / Dan Shafer
      p.  cm.
   Includes index
   ISBN 0-201-48329-7
   1. Macintosh (Computer)    I. Title
QA76.8.M3S529  1995
005.4 ' 3—dc20                                          95–2556
                                                         CIP

Sponsoring Editor: Martha Steffen
Project Manager: John Fuller
Production Coordinator: Ellen Savett
Cover Illustration: Jamie Clay of Digital Phenomena
Cover design: Barbara T. Atkinson
Text design: Vickie Rinehart
Set in 11 point Norvarese by Vickie Rinehart

1 2 3 4 5 6 7 8 9 -DOH- 9998979695
*First printing, April 1995*

Addison-Wesley books are available for bulk purchases by corporations, institutions, and other organizations. For more information please contact the Corporate, Government and Special Sales Department at (800) 238-9682.

This one's for the Golden Goldens—Sandi and CLEO
for fabulous football, fun, and food
Dick for the ping-pong lessons and the cheering section
Michael for the smiles
Glenn for exciting new toys

# CONTENTS

# LIST OF EXERCISES AND EQUIPMENT RULES

# PREFACE

This book is all about how to rid your Macintosh of the dreaded disease known as Disk Bloat. If you're like most Macintosh users, your hard disk somehow never seems to have enough space on it. You have probably become so accustomed to seeing the famous Not Enough Disk Space dialog that you've actually considered inviting it over for lunch. Just last week, you needed to put a full-color scan of your Aunt Tillie on your disk so she'd see her face on your computer and increase your portion of her estate, but there wasn't enough room, which made her mad. Now you're not even *in* her stupid will.

Life with an overcrowded, bloated hard disk is tough. And as multimedia becomes more and more a part of your life, as the Information Superhighway keeps dropping tantalizing little files into your download directory, as applications become suites that eat up more hard disk space than your first computer had altogether, the situation is just going to keep getting worse.

It is clearly time to take up arms against this problem and to stop it before it multiplies. That's what this book is about.

But like any weight-loss program, you won't follow it if it's too strenuous or demanding. So I've carved the process of getting control of your hard drive into a couple dozen easy exercises, each of which will take only a few minutes of your time but will result in some gain. You'll either gain back some hard-fought disk real estate or get some insight into how it gets so bloated to start with, so you can act to prevent it from happening again.

## WHAT ARE WE TRYING TO SAVE?

It seems appropriate at the beginning of our workout together to make sure that we're talking about the same thing. This book is not primarily about how to get more *memory* into your Macintosh. Memory (called RAM, which stands for random access memory and is as arcane a term as you're likely to encounter in this business) certainly gets crowded. But short of adding more hardware to your computer, there's a limit to what you can do to expand the capacity of your computer. (I'll have a few suggestions in Chapter 4, though.)

What we're really going to focus on is your disk drive. You can think of memory as the place where your computer thinks and of the disk drive as the place where it keeps the stuff it thinks about. When you turn off your Macintosh, its memory is entirely erased. But information stored on the disk drive stays there until you remove it—which in the case of many Macintosh owners borders on never. And that's why I decided to write this book.

All of this is made a little confusing by the fact that when you run a program to edit a letter to your boss, for example, your Macintosh copies some of the stuff that's on your hard disk (where it's more or less per- manent, remember) to its memory (where it exists only as long as it needs to and never survives a sys- tem shutdown). So there are actually two copies of that letter: one on the disk and one in your com- puter's memory. When you save the document, you in effect tell your Macintosh, "Put a copy of this letter, which is now in your memory, on the hard disk, where it is safe. Then erase the old copy of the letter." (Actually, sometimes you don't even erase the old copy, as you'll see in Chapter 3.)

So our primary focus is on saving disk space, although we'll have a few exercises designed to give you a little more elbow room in RAM. (Maybe we should have called it Elbow RAM, but there are limits to what my editors will let me get away with here!)

Now that we know *what* we're going to be exercising and making more fit, how will we know how much progress we make? What's the measurement? Pounds, ounces, inches we understand. Even centimeters and meters make some sense to some of us. But what is it that disks have to lose?

Megabytes. (No, that doesn't mean taking a huge chomp out of your favorite chocolate chip cookie.) Megabytes are sometimes abbreviated MB. So what's a megabyte, and what does it mean to free up one of these little suckers on your hard disk?

Let's start with the idea that your computer stores everything, both in RAM and on disks, as 1s and 0s. You've probably heard that before, but you may not have understood entirely what it meant. You can think of this as a kind of code made up of tiny light switches. If a switch is "on," the computer sees it as a 1. If a switch is off, the computer thinks of it as a 0. By combining these 1s and 0s into groups, we can create a code that we can trick the computer into thinking really *means* something. We tell it, for example, "If you see the pattern '01000001,' you should think of that as the letter 'A,'" and it will politely oblige. (Actually, the details are a little more complex, but I'm not trying to make you into a computer scientist here. I couldn't if I wanted to, since I'm not one, either!)

Computer people long ago decided, not entirely arbitrarily, to group these little 1s and 0s (which they call *bits*) into groups of eight (which they call *bytes*.) It takes eight bits to make a byte, and it takes one byte to represent a character or a number.

When you put 1,000 of these bytes together, you get a *kilobyte*, abbreviated either K or KB. Actually, a kilobyte, is 1,024 bytes, for mathematical reasons that only the terminally curious probably care about at this point. Are you with me so far? Good. There's just one more step. If you put 1,000K together, you get—you guessed it!—a *megabyte*, or a million bytes. (Again, the number is actually 1,024,000, for the same mathematical reason.)

So the hard disk on your Macintosh holds a certain number of megabytes of information. Each megabyte is 1,024,000 *characters* (if you'll let me be a little loose about what we define as a character here). Great. And you just read in this morning's newspaper that the national debt is some number of trillions of dollars, and both of these facts make about the same amount of sense to you.

Let's think of it this way. A typical double-spaced page of typing holds about 2,000 characters, give or take a few dozen. So each megabyte on your Macintosh's hard disk can hold the equivalent of something like 5,120 *pages* of text. Now you see why these things

are so valuable in your computing life and why this
Macintosh System Fitness Plan may turn out to be
one of the best investments you ever made.

## WHO CARES IF IT'S CROWDED?

Aside from the fact that you might not have space to
store that incredibly important document because
your hard disk is jam-packed, what are the real consequences of running with an overstuffed hard disk? Why,
in other words, should you care about this problem?

For openers, the issue of running out of space when
you want to put a document on your disk may not be as
trivial as it seems. "No big deal," you might think. "I'll
just remove some of the old stuff cluttering up my disk
and then copy the document again. I don't need a fitness plan or some kind of magic incantation for that."
That is, for the most part, true. But what if the file you
are trying to put on your hard disk is being downloaded
from an electronic bulletin board system or an Internet
location? In that case, you get partway through the file
transfer, and the process stops because you're out of
hard disk space. At a minimum, you lose the time (and
money) associated with the abortive file download. At
worst, you might find yourself in a very long session
while the remote service and your computer keep up a
running argument. "Here's some more file," the remote
system says. "Sorry, I can't take it because I have no
place to put it," your Macintosh replies somewhat coyly.
"Here's some more file." And so it goes, the two computers locked in a sticky variation of the intriguingly
named "fatal embrace" that sometimes happens on
poorly designed networks.

If you are running this kind of download session unattended—in other words, if you're away from the machine while this is going on—your phone line is tied up, and the meter is running while all of this is happening. But quite apart from the issue of just running out of hard disk space during a file transfer or copy, there are other potential problems associated with a bloated hard disk.

Many times when you are working with files on your hard disk, the system needs some spare room to accommodate a request from you or a program. You aren't even aware of the need for this allocation. But its unavailability can make a process impossible to carry out. For example, some programs either allow you to have automatic backup copies of files made as you save documents or need such space as you copy or rename documents. Let's say you have a 2.5MB color graphic of a comet fragment crashing into the surface of Jupiter. You decide to change the resolution of the graphic and, conscious of the scarcity of hard disk space, save it using the same name. The program might well be designed so that it first creates a new document into which to save your changed version and then, only after successfully saving the new version, deletes the original. In that case, if you don't have a reasonable amount of disk space available, you could find yourself in a Catch-22, unable to save the changed document without first exiting and losing the time it took for your Macintosh to redraw the modified graphic.

Because of the way your hard disk works, you might find yourself in a situation in which you need 2.5MB of space for an operation like the one I just described and seem to have it available, but the process still won't work. This may be a result of disk *fragmentation*, a situation in which the available free space on your hard disk is so broken up into smaller pieces that there isn't one chunk big enough to perform some part of an operation. (I'll discuss fragmentation and defragmentation of your hard disk in Chapter 3.)

One final point is worth noting here. Long-time computer users, regardless of the brand of computer they know, strongly recommend that you never have more than 90 percent of your hard disk space occupied. That means, for example, that if you have an 80MB hard disk, you would be well advised to keep at least 8MB free at all times. If you see hard disk space dropping below that 10 percent safety margin, it's time to clean up. (One of the utilities on a special-order disk made just for readers of this book, *Dr. Dan's Macintosh Fitness Plan Disk*, monitors disk usage automatically and lets you know when things are getting marginal.)

## WHAT'S IN THIS BOOK?

This book contains five chapters. Each chapter covers a different aspect of making your Macintosh into a lean, mean computing machine. Within each chapter are several simple exercises: practical, hands-on things you can do to rid your Macintosh of Disk Bloat and make it work more efficiently for you.

Chapter 1 is a kind of warm-up session. Here you'll get a chance to rummage around in your System Folder to find out what's there, what kinds of things might be candidates for later removal, and how to protect yourself against possible pitfalls in the fitness plan scheme. In the process, you'll overcome any barriers you might have as a result of your fear of the unknown.

Chapter 2 begins the real hands-on stuff. In this chapter's exercises, you'll be tossing things liberally into the Trash can on your Macintosh's Desktop as you get rid of documents and files that are unnecessary, duplicated, obsolete, or just plain clutter. You'll also learn a trick for preventing yourself from tossing something away two seconds before you need it. (Never did that in your attic or garage or desk, did you? Naw, not you!)

Chapter 3 moves outside the System Folder and looks at application and document folders strewn about your hard disk drive. Exercises in this chapter focus on finding things that the people who publish software think are way cool but that just occupy space on your hard drive without really contributing much to your Macintosh's well-being.

In Chapter 4, I'll divert a little from the disk space issue and focus briefly on memory and how to expand its availability. To some extent, this discussion is still about disk space, since one of the biggest issues you'll deal with in this chapter is virtual memory. Virtual memory has blurred the distinction between RAM and hard disk space that we spent so much time on at the beginning of this preface. Having more usable memory available can reduce the amount of hard disk space you have to leave available for virtual memory.

Finally, Chapter 5 is our cool-down session; we'll talk about ways to keep things from getting out of hand in the future. The chapter is divided into two main sets of exercises. The first set outlines strategies for managing your hard disk. The second set discusses some of the tools you can obtain to help you figure out if and where you have a problem, and how to prevent and fix such problems.

The book concludes with one appendix, an invaluable listing of the most popular Macintosh programs, along with their file creator types. You'll find this tool extremely helpful as you try to identify orphaned and mysterious documents and files you find in your exploration of your hard disk.

In each chapter, you'll find three kinds of special elements besides the running text:

▶ Exercises, which are hands-on, step-by-step processes for reducing disk bloat

▶ Equipment Rules, which are general principles and techniques that will be used in several places in the book

▶ Tips, which are just what they sound like

Exercises and Equipment Rules are numbered consecutively from the start of the book to the finish, rather than starting over with each chapter. They are listed separately in the Contents and the Index for easy retrieval.

## And Then There's This Disk

As you will by now have discovered, there is no disk firmly attached to the inside back cover of this little volume. The idea is to keep this book small and affordable so that everyone with a Macintosh will feel compelled to buy it. (Pretty sneaky, eh? I almost did not tell you about this, but I figure if you've read this far, you probably already bought the book anyway.)

I have put together a disk that I immodestly call *Dr. Dan's Macintosh Fitness Plan Disk*. There's an order form for this disk at the back of the book. This disk has on it the following programs, which I created specifically for you:

▶ Space Monitor, which keeps an eye on your hard disk's available space and alerts you if it drops to 10 percent of the disk drive's total size or less

▶ Compacting Machine, which helps you set up and maintain a process that will automatically compress, archive, alias, and delete little-used files

▶ Deinstaller, a program you run before and after installing any new software so that if you later want to remove it, you can completely uninstall it rather than leave vestigial traces of it lying around on your hard disk

▶ DupeFinder, which is useful if you're not yet using System 7.5, so that you can easily identify duplicate copies of files and dispose of them appropriately

I'll also throw onto the disk any neat shareware or free-ware utilities I run across from time to time that relate to this issue of keeping your Macintosh lean and fit.

## Contacting the Author

I love hearing from readers. Whether you want to praise or criticize, offer suggestions, or ask me to clarify something that I managed somehow to muddy beyond recognition, please feel free to contact me. The best way to get my attention and a fairly immediate answer is with electronic mail. My preferred address is dshafer@netcom.com. You can also try me on Com-puServe (71246,402) or America OnLine (DSHAFER).

I check those services at least once a day, and I try to answer my e-mail within a day of receiving it. If you don't have electronic mail, you can send me what I affectionately refer to as U.S. Snail Mail at

Dan Shafer, President
The Shafer Group
499 Seaport Ct., Suite 201
Redwood City, CA 94063
Or you can send me a fax at (415) 367-1073.

## Acknowledgments

Everyone who has ever tried to write a book knows that it is at once a solitary and collaborative effort. It is soli-tary in the sense that the author must of necessity spend many hours alone at the word processor, creating the text that people will ultimately read, and that the author must ultimately accept full and unconditional responsibility for the accuracy of the finished work. It is collaborative in the sense that there are always dozens of people who play one role or another, direct or indirect, in the evolution from idea through manuscript to printed books on bookstore shelves.

I owe a debt of gratitude to at least the following people, and would like to acknowledge their contributions. Martha Steffen, Acquisitions Editor at Addison-Wesley, who generated the original idea and saw it through to completion. Bob Pratt of the Boston Computer Society's Macintosh SIG, who contributed virtually all of the Appendix, which I find invaluable and use every day. Guy Mills, technical reviewer, who did an admirable job, particularly in focusing me on System 6 issues that might otherwise have slipped through the cracks. My wife, Carolyn, who read portions of the manuscript, made helpful suggestions, enthused with me about the need for the book, and supported me in all her usually exceptional ways. My editorial assistant, Jeanne Welter, who did her usual sterling job of doing all the stuff I forgot or didn't want to do. The shareware and freeware authors, whose material appears on the disk that you can order using the form at the back of the book, for their contributions to the business of keeping your Mac running soundly. In addition, the following people from Addison-Wesley made contributions to this effort and improved the end product for having touched it: Keith Wollman, Editor-in-Chief; Kaethin Prizer, Editorial Assistant; Vickie Rinehart, Compositor and Designer; John Fuller, Project Manager; Ellen Savett, Production Coordinator; and Barbara Atkinson, Cover Designer.

# THE MACINTOSH SYSTEM FITNESS PLAN

# CHAPTER 1

## INSIDE THE SYSTEM FOLDER

My System Folder is bigger than your System Folder. The problem is, that isn't necessarily as good as having a father (or mother or spouse or even a very good friend) who is bigger than the other person's equivalent protector. In fact, having a big System Folder is a problem. For some of us, it borders on an illness.

When I started writing this book, I had a system with two hard disk drives. On one of them, a 210MB unit, my System Folder occupied 19.2MB. On the other, a 500MB device, the System Folder was 34.9MB. And I'm one of a handful of people left on Planet Earth who remembers the days when 20MB was a big disk drive! The point is that these System Folders were obviously getting out of hand and needed a System Fitness Plan. Badly.

But if you crack open your System Folder (scary though that thought is), you'll probably recognize something less than 20 percent of the stuff in it as things you've put there. You'll probably recognize at least some of the folders, Apple Menu Items, Fonts, Sounds, Control Panels, Extensions, and other items that you have consciously put into your System Folder at various times in your Mac's life.

So where'd the rest of this stuff come from? And, more to the point, do you really need it? How can you tell? What happens if you remove something that sounds unfamiliar to you and then, three months later, you find out that without that weird-sounding file, your monthly budgeting program stubbornly refuses to run at all? It's almost as if someone were secretly feeding your System Folder little fat pills.

In this chapter, I'll teach you how to rummage around in your System Folder, identify candidates for the garbage heap, and avoid shooting yourself in the foot in the process of slimming down your Macintosh's equivalent to your back bedroom closet.

## A BIRD'S-EYE VIEW OF THE SECRET STASH

Alan Mandler, a world-class user interface designer, likes to point to the VCR as perhaps the most poorly designed object with which we come into daily contact. "Almost all of its controls are hidden behind a little door," he points out. "From early childhood, we are taught not to open such doors on penalty of death or mental confusion." So it is with the System Folder. In my Mac travels, I'm continually amazed at how many people have never even opened their System Folders.

So our first exercise is to open this mysterious closet where all sorts of weird-sounding stuff lives and to take a quick tour of how it's organized. (This is more of a warm-up than an exercise, but it's a good place to begin.)

## EXERCISE 1—GETTING TO KNOW YOUR SYSTEM FOLDER

1. Let's find out how overweight your System Folder is. Click on its icon once to highlight it. Now either press Command-I on the keyboard or select Get Info from the File menu in the Finder. A window like the one shown in Figure 1–1 will appear.

**System Folder Info**

System Folder

**Kind :** folder
**Size :** 19.2 MB on disk (19,415,297 bytes used), for 333 items
**Where :** Spinoza :

**Created :** Wed, Sep 14, 1994, 3:33 PM
**Modified :** Tue, Oct 4, 1994, 4:33 PM
**Comments :**

Figure 1–1. Finding out how big your system folder is

2. Note that this dialog tells you not only how many bytes of space your System Folder takes up on your disk but also how many items are contained in it.

3. After recovering from Info Shock, close the window.

4. Open the System Folder by double-clicking on its icon. (Even if you are a System 7 user more

accustomed to turning the little triangular crank next to the folder, this time open it by double-clicking on it. This lets you arrange its view the way you want, independently of how other things on your hard disk are displayed.)

**5.** Go to the Finder's View menu and select By Name, so that the list of applications, folders, and documents in your System Folder appears in alphabetical order.

**6.** If you're using System 7.x, there is at least some semblance of organization here. You'll probably find folders named Apple Menu Items, Control Panels, Extensions, Fonts, and Preferences, among others. If you are running System 6, go to the View menu in the Finder and choose By Kind. This will put all of the objects of the same type together and make it easier to explore this folder. Take a minute to explore your System Folder, getting generally familiar with what's in it. Open some folders. Select an interesting-sounding document and choose Get Info from the File menu. See how many icons you recognize and how many sound totally unfamiliar. Don't worry if you don't understand some or most of it. You'll soon feel quite at home here.

Now that you're comfortable moving around in your System Folder (and have survived your first foray into its mysterious innards), you're ready to do some purposeful exploration.

At this point, take to heart the first rule of working with any computer's files: Back up everything. For the moment, if you will just back up your System Folder to a safe place, you'll give yourself some peace of mind (since you can always recover from an error, so you're less afraid to make one) and security. Also, be sure you have handy a disk from which you can boot your Macintosh in the event of a mistake that disables it. I won't tell you to do anything that would have that result, but you just want to be sure.

> **NOTE:** Take these cautions seriously. They aren't here so this book will be longer. Backing up your data and your system is an important habit to cultivate. If you aren't already doing so, start today!

Let's start with something really easy and safe just to get our feet wet. When the system software was originally installed on your Macintosh, Apple created a number of files for you, including the Scrapbook File. Apple kindly supplies you with some sample artwork in this file. Some of this art may even come in handy someday, but a lot of it is largely useless: empty calories. Let's get rid of some of this stuff.

## EXERCISE 2—TRIMMING USELESS SCRAPBOOK FAT

1. Select the Scrapbook File icon by clicking on it once.

2. Choose Get Info, using either the keyboard or the File menu option. Note its size.

3. Double-click on the Scrapbook File icon. (If you're using System 6, open the Scrapbook from the Apple menu.)

4. Examine each item in the Scrapbook File by scrolling through its contents, using the scrollbar at the bottom of the window. If you can't see the whole object and you want to see it before deciding its fate, copy it and then paste it into your favorite text editor or word processor.

5. When you find an item that you can't see having any real use for (the one shown in Figure 1–2 was one of my favorite candidates for the junk food pile), just use the Edit menu to cut or clear it. (The difference is that Clear removes all traces of the object whereas Cut removes it from its present location and puts a copy on the Clipboard. For all practical purposes, though, they're the same unless you plan to use this object later, in which case you probably shouldn't delete it to begin with!)

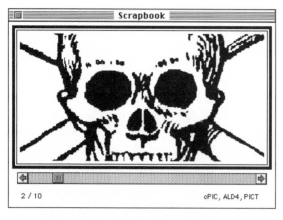

Figure 1–2. Scrapbook File item headed for junk food pile

**6.** After you've eliminated all the useless stuff in your Scrapbook File (and it's perfectly all right to remove everything if you like), close it. The file automatically saves itself.

**7.** Repeat steps 1 and 2 and note how much disk space you've saved. It's probably not much, but every fitness plan starts with a small step toward the ultimate goal of creating a lean, mean machine.

Pretty painless exercise, right? And you gained back some of your previously occupied disk space in the process.

## DEEPER INTO THE RECESSES

In preparation for the serious fitness plan we'll embark on in Chapter 2, let's produce some printouts showing what's in some of the folders that are the most likely candidates for slimming down. This process is easy, but it may be a little time consuming. You should undertake it only when you are ready to work your way through Chapter 2, which will take you between one and three hours, depending on a host of variables. If you have to spread the task over several sessions or days, the folders' contents could change.

If you are using System 6, the process will not be as precise as described in Exercise 3.

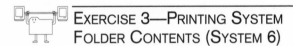

### EXERCISE 3—PRINTING SYSTEM FOLDER CONTENTS (SYSTEM 6)

**1.** Open your System Folder.

**2.** Make sure you are viewing it by name.

**3.** From the File menu, choose Print Directory.

**4.** Repeat the process with any folders contained in your System Folder, as well as any folders contained in those folders, and so on, until you have printed out an alphabetical listing of everything that is in all of the folders in your System Folder.

EXERCISE 3—PRINTING SYSTEM
FOLDER CONTENTS (SYSTEM 7.x)

**1.** Open your System Folder again.

**2.** Look for folders with the names shown in
Table 1–1.

TABLE 1–1. FOLDERS TO LOOK FOR IN SYSTEM FOLDER

| FOLDER NAME | NOTES/COMMENTS |
|---|---|
| Apple Menu Items | Things that appear on your Apple menu |
| Control Panels | Programs and "applets" that extend the functionality of your Macintosh |
| Control Panels (Disabled) | Control panels that have been temporarily disabled because they interfere with something else or are not in use for some other reason |
| Extensions | Programs and "applets" that extend the functionality of your Macintosh |
| Extensions (Disabled) | Extensions that have been temporarily disabled because they interfere with something else or are not in use for some other reason |
| Fonts | Fonts used by all applications |
| Preferences | Covers a multitude of sins, including not only true preferences (files that tell the system how you like certain things to look or behave) but also files and items that installation routines arbitrarily put here |

3. As you find those folders (and you may not have all of them in your System Folder, so don't fret if you don't find one or more of them), open each, make sure you are viewing them by name, and then choose Print Window from the File menu. (The option is called Print Directory in System 6, but the result is the same.)

4. If a particular folder has folders within it, open those in turn, view them by name, and print them as well.

5. When you're done, close all your windows back to the way you like your Desktop to look.

There is a quicker way to print out the contents of your System Folder and of all the folders it contains if you are using System 7. This shortcut results in a single printout with all of the contents displayed. Follow these steps instead of those in Exercise 3:

1. Select the System Folder in the Finder's window for the Startup disk.

2. While holding down the Command and Option keys, press the right-arrow key on your Macintosh keyboard. This keyboard shortcut opens all the folders in a selected folder.

3. Now double-click on the System Folder to open its own window. The Finder remembers that the windows are all open and displays them this way.

**4.** From the File menu, choose Print Window.
(Note that this printout could take a while.)

## FINDING OUT ABOUT SYSTEM FOLDER CONTENTS

The real problem with trying to clean up your System
Folder as we will do in Chapter 2 is figuring out what
in the world a lot of this stuff is. Unless you're unusual, you'll probably find a fair number of objects in
your System Folder that have the icon for plain documents (Figure 1–3) associated with them rather than
an icon that at least gives you a fighting chance to
figure out what they are.

Figure 1–3. Plain document icon

The icon for plain documents is your Macintosh's way
of shrugging, "I don't know where this thing came
from or what application knows how to do anything
with it." When you spot this icon, you know you're
looking at something that is a potential source of
Disk Bloat. Chances are that the application that created this document is no longer on your system. If it
were, your Macintosh would know what kind of icon
to give the object.

NOTE: This general rule about the icon for plain
documents isn't 100 percent reliable. Some
applications, particularly those that aren't
sold commercially, don't bother to create
special icons for the documents they
create. In addition, sometimes your
Macintosh "forgets" what documents go
with what applications and must have its
Desktop rebuilt (by rebooting while you
hold down the Option key to restore the
connection).

Under System 7, the matter of unidentified document
icons became a bit more complex, as Apple Computer
defined several other "generic" document icons, like
the one shown in Figure 1–4 for control panels. Double-
clicking on some icons that look like the one in Figure
1–4 will launch the application to which the document
is connected, but other times, you'll see the by-now-
all-too-familiar dialog that tells you that your Macintosh doesn't know how to open the document.

Figure 1–4. Generic control panel icon

Ultimately, the only way to be certain that a particular document is no longer connected to its application is to double-click on it. If its owning application
can't be found, your system will present the dialog
shown in Figure 1–5.

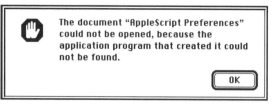

The document "AppleScript Preferences" could not be opened, because the application program that created it could not be found.

OK

Figure 1–5. Orphaned-document dialog

NOTE: Under System 7.5, you will actually see a more meaningful and detailed response in the form of a dialog from which you can identify the application you'd like to use to open the document. The meaning, though, is the same: Your Macintosh is confused and needs human intervention to untangle itself.

Sometimes you will see a perfectly clear, nongeneric icon on your system but find that its parent application can't be located. Not all disconnected documents display the generic icon.

Often, a file's name gives you a pretty clear indication of the application to which it's connected. Documents named Word Temp followed by a number, for example, are clearly Microsoft Word documents. The AppleScript Preferences file I tried to open in Figure 1–5 obviously belongs to AppleScript. If all developers were so considerate as to name their files in a way that you could connect them mentally to the right product, life would be much simpler. Unfortunately, that's not the case.

As we'll see in Chapter 2, it's important to identify, if
at all possible, the application connected to a document you're not sure you need. If the document's icon
and name give you no clues and if you just can't remember (or, more likely, never knew) the application
yourself, there is one more way to find out.

If you have a copy of ResEdit on your system, you can
use it to determine the creator of a particular document in many cases. (If you don't have ResEdit, you
may want to get it, particularly if your system is
plagued with lots of this particular specie of Bloat
Beast. You can obtain it on popular electronic bulletin
board systems in the book *ResEdit Complete* by Peter
Alley and Carolyn Strange (Addison-Wesley, 1991).

Assuming you have ResEdit, you can find out which
application created a particular document by following these steps:

   **1.** Launch ResEdit.

   **2.** If necessary, cancel the opening dialog.

   **3.** From the File menu, choose Get File/Folder Info.

   **4.** Navigate to the document you want to analyze
   and choose it.

   **5.** The resulting dialog looks like the one in
   Figure 1–6. Note the entry labeled Creator. All
   Macintosh applications are supposed to have a
   unique four-character creator code that they
   associate with the documents they create and

understand. In theory, at least, these codes are registered by the developer with Apple Computer, Inc., to ensure that they aren't duplicated. In practice, this isn't always the case. Sometimes the code is sufficiently well chosen so that it tells you which program created a document without any further effort on your part. If the code doesn't seem familiar or obvious, you can refer to the appendix to help you. The appendix contains the creator codes for the most popular programs on the Macintosh as registered with Apple Developer Services or discovered by Mac users.

NOTE: You can repeat steps 3 and 4 as many times as you like. You can also close these windows if things get too cluttered.

---

| Info for Chapter 1 |
|---|

File: | Chapter 1|                                    ☐ Locked

Type: | WDBN |    Creator: | MSWD |

☐ File Locked          ☐ Resources Locked          File In Use: Yes
☐ Printer Driver MultiFinder Compatible    File Protected: No

Created: | Sat, Oct 22, 1994 |    Time: | 10:49:00 AM |

Modified: | Thu, Dec 15, 1994 |    Time: | 12:51:13 PM |

Size:        0 bytes in resource fork
             64000 bytes in data fork

Finder Flags: ◉ 7.x ○ 6.0.x

☐ Has BNDL      ☐ No INITs      Label: | None    ▼ |
☐ Shared        ☒ Inited        ☐ Invisible
☐ Stationery    ☐ Alias         ☐ Use Custom Icon

Figure 1–6. ResEdit's file info window

ResEdit won't always be helpful, because too often
developers forget the little detail of either assigning
their creator types to such documents or using a
generic creator like "ttxt" (which is Apple's own Teach-
Text program) because their Preference file or other
document can be read by TeachText. Ultimately, you
sometimes just can't figure out what application
hooks up to a particular document.

## SUMMARY OF KEY TECHNIQUES

In this chapter, you learned the following useful techniques for putting your Macintosh on a fitness plan:

▶ Selecting a folder or icon and using the Finder's
   Get Info capability to find out how big it is (and
   other data about it that will be useful later)

▶ Identifying potential orphaned documents by
   their icons

▶ Using ResEdit to find out the creator of a
   document

# CHAPTER 2

# CLEANING UP YOUR SYSTEM'S ACT

O kay, people, time to clean house! In this chapter, we'll get serious about this slimming-down regime we're prescribing for our Macintosh systems.

A wise man once told me that when you have a job to do, start with the hardest, nastiest, most obnoxious part. When that's done, the rest of the job will look like a piece of cake. Candidly, that hasn't always worked all that well for me, but it still *seems* like good advice. So let's start with the deep, dark mysterious recesses of your System Folder. Once we're done with that, the rest of the bloat your system has picked up over the years will seem like child's play by comparison. Trust me.

In Chapter 1, we peeked inside the System Folder to get a general idea of what's there. Now we're going to dig more deeply into this Mystery of Mysteries and see how many things we can find to toss into the proverbial bit bucket. Along the way, we'll inevitably be drawn outside the System Folder into application folders elsewhere on your hard disk to look for systemlike documents and objects that are candidates for removal.

## PRELIMINARIES

To begin your workout, make sure you have a current printout of the contents of your System Folder. You created one of these in Exercise 3 in Chapter 1, but if

any significant amount of time has passed since you
did that, it's a good idea to produce a new one. As
we'll see shortly, strange objects have a way of appearing in your System Folder when you're not looking.

At this point, you might well want to make a list of
the applications you use most often and where they
are located on your disk drive. Keep this list handy
throughout this chapter's workout. (You might also
want to browse the list of Macintosh applications in
the appendix. You might have overlooked something
that you use infrequently, but often enough that it
might prove important as you rummage around in the
System Folder attic.)

Since we're going to be looking at various document,
application, and system extension objects, it will be
helpful to be sure they are "in synch" with your hard
disk's current state. For arcane reasons, your Macintosh sometimes "forgets" what application is connected to a particular document, for example. This
sometimes leads to the presence of the uninforma-
tive generic-document icon we learned about in
Chapter 1. To reduce the number of those lying
around in your System Folder as much as possible,
we're going to rebuild the Desktop on your Mac before we start our serious workout plan.

> NOTE: Rebuilding your Desktop is a very safe
> activity. In fact, Apple Computer support
> personnel have been known to recommend
> that you make it a practice to rebuild your

Desktop every few weeks. But rebuilding your Desktop has one unfortunate side effect: All of the comments associated with files are deleted when you rebuild your Desktop. It's not likely that this is a big deal, but if it is, you have two choices. Either find a way to avoid losing the comments or don't rebuild your Desktop. This step isn't mandatory, but it will probably make things a bit easier.

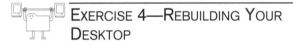

## EXERCISE 4—REBUILDING YOUR DESKTOP

1. Start this exercise with your Macintosh turned off.

2. Turn your Macintosh on.

3. Hold down the Command and Option keys as your system starts up. Keep them held down until you see a dialog box like the one shown in Figure 2–1.

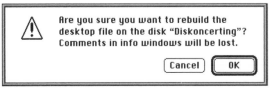

Figure 2-1. Dialog box for rebuilding Desktop

**4.** Click on the OK button.

**5.** The system will rebuild your startup drive's
Desktop. If you have other hard disks available
at the time you perform this exercise, you'll be
asked in turn whether you want to rebuild their
Desktops as well. It's probably not necessary,
but it doesn't hurt anything, either. You can
decide. (Isn't that charitable of me?)

---

With your Desktop rebuilt, your system now knows as
much as it can about what documents or files go with
what applications. That will take some of the guess-
work out of the rest of our workout.

In the interest of being as cautious as possible, let's
take one more step and put into effect the Extra-Safe
Way Out. Create a folder in your System Folder and
name it something like Toss Out 7/1/95 or something
similar. (Note: You can put two spaces in front of the
folder name so that it will appear at or near the top of
the alphabetical listing of System Folder contents.
You don't have to follow that convention, of course.)
If you have any hesitation about whether throwing
away a particular object is going to be safe, you can
put that object into this folder. That way, if you discover later that you wish you hadn't thrown it away, it
will still be there. (Of course, you *did* remember to
back it up before all of this fun started, didn't you?)

Be sure to clean out this folder, though. It's probably safe to assume that if you haven't used a document in a few weeks, you probably don't need it.

> **NOTE:** Another way of giving yourself this extra protection is with a shareware program called TrashMan. This handy little utility automates Trash emptying and allows you to decide how long files should be held in the Trash before being deleted. This program is on the Dr. Dan's Macintosh System Fitness Plan disk you can order using the coupon at the back of this book.

## FINDING FILES

If you're using System 6, you have probably used the Find File desk accessory Apple includes with the system. Find File is a marginally useful tool that searches a specific disk for a specific text string.

With System 7, Apple decided that a program called the Finder ought to do at least a little intelligent finding, so it improved the capability considerably. System 7.5 adds even further capabilities.

To find a file under System 7, just select the Find option from the File menu in the Finder. The result will be a dialog like the one in Figure 2–2 under System 7.5. The dialog in System 7.1 is less attractive but functionally nearly identical.

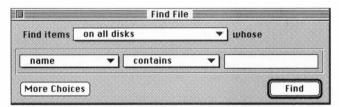

Figure 2-2. Find File dialog, System 7.5 edition

You can select which disks or locations to search,
which field to search, and whether to look for files
that start with, end with, contain, or otherwise match
or don't match the criteria you provide. The More
Choices button expands the dialog in System 7.5 and
opens a new one in System 7.1. Both provide you with
some additional ways to conduct searches.

If you find the functionality of the built-in Find opera-
tions too limited, you can purchase a commercial
Desk Accessory with more capability. Two of the best
are Alki Seek, from Alki Software Corp., and Fast Find,
from Symantec Corp.

## THE OUTER LIMITS

Begin your System Folder trimming exercises by focusing just on the objects that appear at its top level,
that is, not inside other folders. There shouldn't be a
lot of items at this level; if there are, they probably
need some organization. But that's beyond the scope
of this book. (I promised to get your system slim and
trim, not organized, after all.)

NOTE: If you're using System 6, your System Folder's organization is radically different from what I'll be describing. Most of the documents and other objects I'll describe here are stored either at the top level of the System Folder or, in most cases, in the System icon itself. The *principles* regarding what to consider eliminating are valid, but finding the objects won't be the same. I'll note where there are differences that I can predict, but on some level, you'll have to use this chapter as a general guide to dealing with System Bloat in System 6.

Look at each item that isn't in a folder. Apply to each item Equipment Rule 1.

## EQUIPMENT RULE 1—ANALYZING OBJECTS

Apply this process any time you are evaluating an object to determine whether it should stay on your disk.

### Phase One: Identification

1. Do you recognize its icon or its name? If so, move to the next phase, Deciding What to Do with It.

**2.** If you don't recognize its icon or its name, use Get Info. Sometimes even a generic-document icon will reveal the originating application, even after you've rebuilt your Desktop.

**3.** If Get Info is no help, use ResEdit as described briefly in Chapter 1 to find out its creator ID and use this information to attempt to identify the object from the appendix or other resources.

**4.** If can't identify the object, use the Extra-Safe Way Out folder rather than tossing it directly into Trash.

**Phase Two: Deciding What to Do with It**

Having identified the object, decide what to do with it, using this process:

**1.** Ask yourself if it belongs with an application you use often or need to keep around even for occasional use. (If you answer yes, you can stop evaluating this one; it's a keeper.)

**2.** Are you sure you don't need it? (Toss it.)

**3.** If you're not sure, use the Extra-Safe Way Out folder rather than tossing it directly into Trash.

> TIP: As you go through the System Folder workout
>       in this chapter, you might find it helpful to
>       keep the printout of the folder that you
>       created at the outset close at hand. You can
>       then mark off each object as you look at it.
>       Particularly if you break this workout into
>       smaller sessions, this will prove quite helpful.

## PRODUCT-SPECIFIC FOLDERS

After you've sifted through the top-level documents
and objects in your System Folder, it's time to do
some drilling. You could take the folders in alphabetical order, but it turns out that there are some patterns
of folder types that have some things in common. As a
result, working through the folders in a more logical
sequence pays some benefits in efficiency.

Start with the product-specific folders. These folders
usually bear names that reveal the application to
which they are related: Aladdin, Claris, Eudora, XTND
(Claris technology), GlobalFax, and the like.

You'll find that some of these folders have other folders nested inside of them. Treat these nested folders
just like the product-specific folders themselves.

### WHAT YOU SHOULD LOOK FOR
Several kinds of files that are good candidates for
removal are often found in product-specific folders.
The most common kinds are:

▶ Tutorial and sample documents

▶ Templates to be used to create specific
document types

▶ Translators and converters

▶ Telecommunication program modem drivers
(CCLs)

We'll take a look at each of these types of documents,
sometimes grouping similar types together for discussion purposes.

### Tutorials, Samples, and Templates

Software publishers have not been consistent in
placing tutorial, sample, and template (stationery)
documents in the System Folder. Sometimes they
place such folders in the application folders directly.
The principles set forth in this section are valid regardless of where you ferret out these often unnecessary files, however helpful they might be
temporarily or to a user with a different set of needs
and interests.

### EXERCISE 5—SEARCHING OUT TUTORIAL FILES

Some applications include tutorial documents and
lesson materials that are useful when you are learning them but that are largely uninteresting after
you've mastered the product. Unfortunately, these
files are often quite large because they include lots of

detailed instructions, varieties of objects with which to work, and so forth. Let's see if there are any files of this type in your project-specific folders.

1. Open a product-specific folder so you can see the folders and documents it contains.

2. Scan through the names of the folders for such words as Tutorial, Introductory, and Learning. If you spot any such folders or documents, investigate their contents and decide whether you think you will be likely to need them. If not, these are great candidates for elimination. (Assuming you know where the original diskettes are, you can safely toss these documents and folders, since the application won't depend on their being around.)

3. You can repeat the first two steps for objects that are not exactly tutorials but that serve a similar purpose. For example, some word processing and spreadsheet programs include a great many sample documents that are designed to give you ideas and starting points for creating your own documents. This is very helpful, but if you're not likely ever to need to create a construction cost estimate, having a spreadsheet example or template file that makes that task easier isn't really of much use.

> **TIP:** Many tutorial and sample documents are either stored as stationery documents or are locked so that you don't inadvertently change them and erase their value. When you try to throw these documents away, you may find yourself being told that some items couldn't be deleted because they were locked or in use. Just hold down the Option key as you empty the Trash, and this problem will disappear. So will the files!

For example, if you have installed ClarisWorks you'll find a folder called ClarisWorks Stationery, which has the following documents:

- ▶ ABOUT Stationery

- ▶ Business Stationery

- ▶ Fax Cover Sheet

- ▶ Internal Memorandum

- ▶ Mail Merge Letter

- ▶ Name & Address-Standard

- ▶ Newsletter-WP

- ▶ Personal Stationery-Std.

▶ Presentation-Outline

▶ To-Do-List-Outline

You can tell from the names of these documents whether they will be useful templates for things you might want to create. If you never expect to be called on to design and lay out a newsletter, you can certainly toss that one, for example. These documents are typically about 40K in size; eliminating a half dozen of them gains you a quarter of a megabyte of space.

## Translators

Many programs provide you with a number of files whose purpose is to help you import files created using other tools. There can be a staggering array of these file translators. The chances that you'll actually use more than a small handful of them are pretty slim unless you're in an unusual business such as publishing, where you have to be ready to accept files from word processors to which stubborn writers cling long after improved products have become available.

(Don't misunderstand. It is admirable that these publishers make such translators available. For several years after the Macintosh appeared on the market, converting documents between applications—even those that ran on the Macintosh, let alone between Microsoft Windows and the Macintosh—was painful if not impossible. But you are in a better position to decide which, if any, translators you actually need occupying space on your disk.)

Deciding which translators or converters to keep
requires a little thought. Here's an exercise that can
result in gaining better control of this aspect of
your system.

## EXERCISE 6—UNCOVERING
## TRANSLATORS AND CONVERTERS

1. Refer to your list of the applications you use
   frequently. Ask yourself how often, if at all, you
   need to translate whole documents from one
   application's format to another. (Remember
   that you can often copy and paste small
   amounts of information between programs.
   Remember, too, that if the applications support Publish-and-Subscribe (System 7.x or
   later), you often don't need to handle any specific document conversion outside that
   process.)

2. Now make a list of any applications your col-
   leagues, customers, and others use and from
   which you have to translate documents.

3. Consider the question of whether you need
   two-way compatibility or whether you typically
   need only to import or export specific document formats.

4. Armed with this information, locate the con-
   verter or translator files within your product-
   specific folders. They are typically pretty clearly
   named to reflect their capability. Any that you

find that you aren't fairly certain you need are
candidates for the junk food pile.

---

These files are often 60–128K in size, so finding a few
unnecessary examples of translators or converters
can result in picking up a megabyte fairly quickly. The
Claris Translators file installed with ClarisWorks 2.1,
for example, has thirty-three translators that occupy a
total of 813K on your disk.

NOTE: If you find yourself doing frequent
translations involving a variety of file
formats, you might want to consider
purchasing a product designed to handle
such a task. For example, LapLink, from
Traveling Software, offers dozens of file
format compatibilities between
Macintoshes and across Windows-
Macintosh links. These are often not only
more efficient and effective translators
than those that come with word
processors, spreadsheets, databases, and
telecommunications programs, but also
often take up less disk space. These
specialized programs often have custom
installation routines that let you select
only those translators you really need.

## Modem Drivers

If you have any telecommunications programs or integrated packages that include such products (for example, ClarisWorks or Microsoft Works), there is at least a chance that you have a veritable gold mine of opportunity for shedding excess system weight.These programs typically install modem drivers (known as CCLs) in sometimes staggering numbers.

Unless you plan to change modems in the near future without changing terminal software, you probably don't need more than one of the CCLs in your System Folder. Assuming, of course, that your telecommunications program is working well with your present hardware, you can simply identify which CCL you're using and delete all of the others. Don't forget that you may be using the program with more than one modem if you have a PowerBook that you carry frequently between home and office.

NOTE: Sometimes your telecommunications program stores the CCLs it uses in its application folder rather than in your System Folder. That's how all of these programs *should* behave. But Macintosh programmers have learned that if they put things into your System Folder, you're much less likely even to *see* them, let alone wonder about them and possibly even (perish the thought) delete them. Sometimes these concerns are legitimate.

> More often, though, they're just the safest,
> easiest way for programmers to make
> programs work the way they expect them
> to work.

The first thing you have to do is find where the telecommunications program you are using keeps its
CCLs. This isn't always as straightforward as it seems.
Many telecom programs store their CCLs in your System Folder. Others keep them in their own folder,
perhaps in a folder that is logically named or perhaps
not. In fact, not all telecom programs even have CCL
files. The widely popular shareware program ZTerm,
for example, doesn't use the CCL approach at all.
Rather, it provides menus with which you can cus-
tomize the telecom interactions it holds with other
computers. It recognizes that you use only one
modem at a time and simply allows you to configure
it. The bad news is, configuring it isn't trivial if you
don't have at least a rudimentary working knowledge
of telecommunications terminology.

### EXERCISE 7—IDENTIFYING THE MODEM DRIVER YOU ARE USING

1. Launch the telecommunications program you
   are using.

2. Look for a menu option called something like
   Modem Setup or Modem Options or just Setup.
   The name may be some variation on this theme,

so you may have to do a little digging. (Of course if your program is like ZTerm and doesn't use CCLs, this whole exercise is fruitless.)

3. In the dialog box displayed after you select the appropriate menu entry, there is probably a popup menu that lists all the modems this program "knows" about (those that have CCLs defined for it). Note the name of the driver that is now selected (it's the one showing in the popup before you select it). Write that name down for later reference.

4. If your program doesn't have such a setup dialog or for some other reason you can't find the name of the CCL the program uses with your modem, you can use the technique in Exercise 8 for identifying the appropriate driver(s) to keep.

5. Quit your telecom program. (You may in fact have to do this before you can delete any of the CCLs associated with your program, because the program may not allow you to delete those files while it is running.)

---

There is no common terminology for what the folders that hold CCLs are called, so finding where these little beasties are stored is what programmers call a "nontrivial task." But there is a single shortcut that will work in 99 percent of cases.

## EXERCISE 8—FINDING AND REMOVING MODEM CCL FILES

1. If you've already identified the CCL file(s) you need to keep, skip to step 6.

2. From the Finder, choose the Find option under the File menu.

3. Depending on what version of the system you are using, use the appropriate technique to find files whose names contain the word Hayes.

NOTE: D. C. Hayes was a pioneering company in the modem business and for years dominated the market for personal computer–based telecommunications devices. It became customary for all modems to achieve "Hayes compatibility." As a result, it is virtually unheard of for any file of CCLs not to include at least one Hayes driver or a driver labeled something like Hayes Compatible.

4. Use the result of this Find operation to locate the folder(s) where CCLs are stored on your system.

5. Navigate to each of those folders in turn.

6. In each folder that contains CCLs, identify the one (or more) associated with your modem needs. Generally, this is easy because the CCLs

have names that identify the modem(s) with which they are designed to work. Be careful, though, because there are two possible "gotchas" here. First, there may be more than one CCL for your modem if it needs a different CCL for different speeds (baud rates) and protocols (for example, V.32 or V.42). Second, your modem may not be supported by the software, or your driver may not be the one installed for the program for some reason. The next steps address what to do in these situations; if they don't apply to you, skip to step 8.

7. If there are multiple CCLs for your modem, you can probably err on the side of safety and keep them all. As I said earlier, they are pretty small, so a few of them hanging around on your hard disk isn't going to be a big problem. Just toss the other drivers that are clearly not needed.

8. If in steps 2–4 you can't figure out with the Find technique which CCL your program is using you might try seeing if it's using a generic modem driver. These drivers have names like Hayes

NOTE: I recommend keeping these generic-sounding CCLs around. They can come in handy in case your normal CCL fails to work for some reason. You can sometimes get your telecom program to work with one of these generic routines until you can figure out the problem.

Basic, Hayes Compatible, or Generic Modem. Scan for one of those in the folder with which you're working.

9. Because these files are small but crucial and because reinstalling them can sometimes be a pain in the modemus maximus, I'd suggest you put all of the drivers you suspect you don't need but are not 100 percent sure about into the Extra-Safe Way Out folder. Then launch your program and be sure you can still connect.

---

Finding and removing the unused CCLs in your system can pay big dividends for your Macintosh's fitness, even though individually these files tend to be small, almost always under 20K. The reason? There are so many of them lying around. For example, America OnLine, one of my favorite telecom hot spots, stores all of its CCLs in a folder called Online Files, which it stores in its own folder. There are something on the order of 115 of these files, and their combined Disk Bloat rating is a not inconsiderable 700K. Removing all but the one or two you need can save you the equivalent of half a floppy of disk space on your hard drive.

## SCREEN SAVER IMAGES

If you have a screen saver like Berkeley Systems' After Dark installed on your system—and it's a safe bet that you do, since the vast majority of Macintosh systems on desktops use these programs—you should enjoy the benefits of this exercise.

## EXERCISE 9—SHEDDING EXCESS SCREEN SAVER MODULE WEIGHT

**1.** Scan through your System Folder and look for folders whose names indicate that they contain screen saver files. Most screen savers store their images in a folder in the System Folder. If you don't see anything at the top level, check out the Preferences, Extensions, and Control Panels folders.

**2.** When you locate this folder, open it.

**3.** You'll probably be surprised at the number and variety of modules stored in this folder. Some of them are pretty large, too.

**4.** If you're not sure what a particular image looks like, you can launch the screen saver program by double-clicking on its icon and then using its preview or demo capabilities to look at the individual images you want to examine.

**5.** You'll almost certainly find at least a few images here that just don't appeal to you. You might identify one or two that you've never seen before that you think are really cool, too.

**6.** Once you've identified all of these images that you're unlikely ever to want to use on your system, mercilessly herd them into the Trash can.

### SOME GENERAL CLOSING ADVICE

When you are rummaging about in application-specific folders in the System Folder, keep your eyes open and your curiosity detector turned on high. If you see a document or a folder that you don't think sounds useful, explore it. Find out how big it is; that will help you decide if it's worth spending any significant amount of time figuring out what it is.

If you wind up terminally curious about something, stick it into the Extra-Safe Way Out folder and then run the application to see if there's anything critical in the folder. The worst that *should* happen is that the program won't run. Then you'll know that the folder or document is critical, and you can just put it back where you got it. No harm done.

Remember, it's *your* system, not Microsoft's, not Claris's, not America OnLine's, not anyone's but yours. Be bold!

### SYSTEM-LEVEL FOLDERS

When you are working with all of the folders in your System Folder that are not obviously related to a specific program, you need to be a bit more careful than with application folders. Still, you can almost always safely put items you suspect of causing Disk Bloat into the Extra-Safe Way Out folder and then run for a while to see if any dire consequences result. Usually you'll know right away because the system won't run or some common function will suddenly stop working.

We'll start our exploration by poking around in some folders that you're almost certainly going to find in your System Folder because virtually every Macintosh has them. Then we'll offer some general suggestions and exercises that are less specific to individual folders.

> **NOTE:** The Macintosh helps you organize your System Folder under System 7.5 much more proactively than under System 7.1 or System 6. In System 7.5, folders provide default homes for many kinds of documents and files. I'll be assuming here that you are using System 7.5. If you aren't, you may have to use a little imagination to find the same kinds of files I'm describing as belonging in a particular folder. I'll help out where I can, but this level of organization in System 7.5 is one of the best and least-appreciated reasons for upgrading to it if you haven't.

### FONTS

Don't tell my wife I'm even *suggesting* that you remove any fonts from your system. She believes that you can never be too rich, too beautiful, or have too many fonts. When she opens the Font menu in her version of Microsoft Word, the menu takes about three minutes to open completely on her big screen. It's a sight to behold.

The fact is, unless you're a desktop publisher, a graphics artist, or a kidnapper who needs a well-disguised ransom note now and then, you almost certainly have more fonts on your system than you're ever going to use. And these things take up *gobs* of space; they are among the biggest causes of Disk Bloat.

 ## EXERCISE 10—FINDING AND REMOVING UNUSED FONTS

**1.** Before you can get rid of unneeded fonts, you need to figure out where your system has stashed them. Table 2–1 gives you the primary places to look, depending on the version of the system you are using.

TABLE 2–1. POSSIBLE FONT LOCATIONS

| SYSTEM VERSION | TOP LEVEL OF FOLDER | FONTS FOLDER | INSTALLED IN SYSTEM |
|---|---|---|---|
| 6 | | | √ |
| 7.1 | √ | | √ |
| 7.5 | √ | √ | √ |

**2.** Font files have four possible icons, two of which are common and important to know. Fonts sometimes appear in suitcases with the letter "A" on them (see Figure 2–3). This suitcase object can contain either TrueType fonts (which you can think of as "smart" or "sophisticated" fonts that know how to draw themselves on your screen and printer smoothly) or bitmapped fonts (also known as "screen fonts). The icon for

a bitmapped or screen font is a document icon
with the letter "A" occupying most of the icon
(see Figure 2–3). The other font icons represent
a TrueType font and a Postscript font and are
less prevalent today (although Postscript fonts
are required if you run either Adobe Type Manager or Adobe Acrobat).

Courier        GaramBol

Figure 2–3. Icons for fonts

**3.** If you find one or more fonts you're pretty sure
you can do without, you'll need to be sure that
only the Finder is running before you try to remove them. If you forget to do this, the system
will remind you (System 7.x) with a dialog like
the one in Figure 2–4.

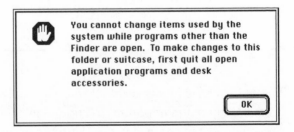

Figure 2–4. Dialog response to attempting to delete
font with applications open

**4.** Don't delete the fonts named Chicago, Helvetica,
Monaco, New York, and Times, since these are
considered "base" fonts that are often used in

documents provided by publishers of various Macintosh programs to display instructions. Chicago is a system font used in dialog boxes, menus, and dozens of other places, for example. Also, if you have changed the font used to display your document and folder names in the Finder, don't remove the font you're using for that purpose.Other than those restrictions, feel free to toss any font that doesn't seem like you're likely to use it. (You *did* back up your system before you started this, didn't you?)

**TIP:** Under System 7.x, you can double-click on a font's icon and see what it looks like even if you aren't using it in any program at the moment. The dialog looks like Figure 2–5.

Figure 2–5. Displaying a font from the Finder

If you are using System 7, you may find a folder called
Fonts (Disabled) in your System Folder. If you find a
folder of that name and it has fonts in it, they've
probably been there long enough now that you've
been unaware of them and you can safely toss these.

### SOUNDS

Sounds are less likely to proliferate on your disk, if
only because most programs you buy don't have any
sounds associated with them. (As multimedia gains
prominence, however, this situation is bound to
change.) On the other hand, some sound files are
*huge*, so finding them and removing unnecessary
noises and sound effects can pay big dividends as
you pump up your lean, mean Mac machine.

Sound files, whose icon looks like a speaker (see
Figure 2–6), are usually stored directly in the system
itself. Any sound you want to use as the system's
"beep" sound must be stored in the system. Sounds
used by other programs are usually stored in the
specific application folders.

Figure 2–6. Sound file icon

### EXERCISE 11—FINDING AND REMOVING UNWANTED SOUNDS

1. Close all applications, control panels, and desk
   accessories, leaving only the Finder open.

**2.** Find the suitcase-shaped icon named System in your System Folder.

**3.** Double-click on that icon. The result should look something like Figure 2–7. As you can see, the Finder holds primarily fonts and sounds.

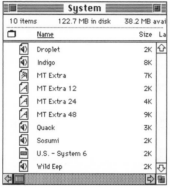

| Name | Size | La |
|------|------|-----|
| Droplet | 2K | |
| Indigo | 8K | |
| MT Extra | 7K | |
| MT Extra 12 | 2K | |
| MT Extra 24 | 4K | |
| MT Extra 48 | 9K | |
| Quack | 3K | |
| Sosumi | 2K | |
| U.S. - System 6 | 2K | |
| Wild Eep | 2K | |

System — 10 items — 122.7 MB in disk — 38.2 MB avai

Figure 2–7. Inside the System icon

**NOTE:** The System icon in System 6 holds much more than sounds and fonts. In System 6, most of the extensions you made to the system were stored in this icon. Also, under System 6 you cannot double-click on the icon System and open it. Instead, you must use Font/DA Mover, a program Apple Computer supplied with your system to relocate any item stored in the system.

**4.** Identify sounds that you don't intend to use as system sounds.

5. Move these sounds either to the Trash or to your Extra-Safe Way Out folder.

6. After you've cleaned up the sound act in your system, you can safely restart applications you may have had to quit to start this exercise.

---

### PRINTERS PROLIFERATE

How many times have you opened the Chooser (see Figure 2–8) and wondered how in the world you ended up with icons representing every printer known to MacLand? But then you just select the printer you need to get that report out by 5:00 P.M. and forget about going back later to see what is going on here.

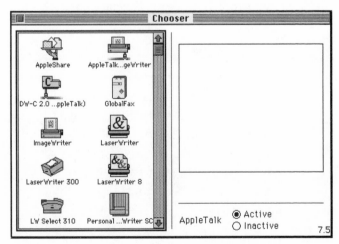

Figure 2–8. Chooser for Printers

Let's do another little exercise to tighten up the system's fitness on the printer front.

## Exercise 12—Removing Unused Printers

1. Open the Extensions folder in your System Folder. This is where printer drivers are stored under System 7. (If you're using System 6 you'll find them at the top level of the System Folder.)

2. Identify the printer(s) you use with this system.

3. Scroll through the Extensions folder and select all of the printers you don't use, don't expect to buy, never heard of, and can't imagine why they exist.

4 Toss those printers into the old Trash can.

### System Capabilities You'll Never Use

When a system is installed on your Macintosh, a fairly significant number of files you'll almost certainly never use get put into your System Folder. If you're like most Macintosh users, you've never wanted to move these files for fear of breaking something.

Most of these "goodies" end up in the Extensions folder or the Control Panels folder. Open those folders and see if anything sounds like something you're not likely to find a use for. Here are some of my personal favorites, but don't let this list be limiting:

▶ Easy Access. This extension makes your system easier to use if you have a physical challenge.

Apple should be applauded heartily for including this kind of capability in the system. And if
you're using these features, by all means leave
them in place. But if you don't need them, you
can safely toss this little item.

▶ Voice Record. Some people love playing around
with recording their own voices on their Macintoshes. I have a friend who has used his own
voice and a popular shareware program called
Sound Manager to modify his system so that
warning messages and alert notifications all
come out sounding like him talking to himself.
Public rumor to the contrary, I'm not particularly enamored of my own voice. I tossed this
162K Disk Bloater thirty seconds after I ran
across it.

▶ PowerBook. If you're on a desktop machine, this
goodie is about as useless a device as you're
likely to run across.

In general, my advice here is the same as you've
heard before. If you run across something that
sounds vaguely useless or uninteresting, stuff it into
your Extra-Safe Way Out folder for a few days or
weeks to see if anything untoward happens. If not,
pitch that item. You can always go back and recover it
with a custom installation of your system software.

## DISABLED ITEMS

The longer you've been using your Macintosh, the
more likely it is that you'll find two folders in your
System Folder that bear a strong resemblance to the

old Fibber McGee's closet of 1930s radio fame. These folders are Extensions (Disabled) and Control Panels (Disabled).

How do items get into these folders? Most of the time, you put them there. Sometimes you do it knowingly, and other times you are just answering a question posed by some program and it takes care of the messy work for you.

If you haven't even looked into these folders in the past few months, you're almost certainly safe simply to open them up and shake their moldy, dusty contents directly into the Trash bin. After all, if you haven't needed them in so long you've forgotten what they are, you probably don't need them.

Since these objects are already in a disabled state, it isn't necessary for you to put them into your Extra-Safe Way Out folder; if you're done with them, toss them. No sense cluttering up the old Mac system waistline with really empty calories.

## ELIMINATING DUPLICATE FILES

Duplicate files can end up in your System Folder— and elsewhere on your hard disk—in a number of different ways. For example, you might install a program and then later either install the same version inadvertently into a different folder or install a full upgrade without deleting the original. Another way you can wind up with duplicate files results from the fact that some programs assume that you don't have

some requisite file and install their own copies or
versions of files that already exist as a result of other
program installations you undertook earlier.

Programs that involve the Apple Comm Toolbox
seem to have a nasty tendency to proliferate. One of
my hard disks had three sets of several of these tools
when I started writing this book. With the Information Super Cowpath...er, Highway...looming on your
personal horizon, these files are going to be worth
checking on!

However they occur, duplicate files obviously waste
disk space. But before you run off and find all the
duplicate files on your hard drive and blow them into
the bit bucket, there is one major consideration to
take into account.

Some programs expect to find certain files in certain
places. Even though you might have two copies of the
same file in your System Folder, the programs that
may use these files may need to look for them in different places. So the mere fact of their duplication
isn't sufficient grounds for excising them from your
System Folder's life.

This is a clear case for the use of the Extra-Safe Way
Out folder. Before permanently disposing of the files
you will want to identify the programs that use the
duplicated files, put apparently unneeded copies of
the files into the safety folder, and then run the applications in question to be sure they still run correctly.

### FINDING THE DUPLICATES

One way to find duplicate files is to use the printout of the System Folder's contents you prepared as part of the preliminaries for this chapter. You can probably spot duplicate files there just by scanning the list repeatedly.

When you find duplicate files, mark them (using color highlighters is helpful in this process). Then you can go to your Macintosh and start determining which, if any, of these files are actually identical twins and which are different versions of a file.

NOTE: You have to be a little careful here. It would not be unheard of, for example, for you to find three documents with the word Dictionary in their names. Yet all might be completely different dictionaries, used by different applications. Removing one or two of these seemingly duplicated files prematurely could cause the spelling function in your favorite word processor or desktop presentation package to refuse to work next time you try it. Such fake duplicates will almost certainly have different icons.

Besides a visual scan of the printout of the System Folder's contents, you can use more automated techniques for identifying duplicate files in System 7.

(The Finder in System 6 lacked a true "find" capability, so this support isn't available if you're running on System 6.)

## EXERCISE 13—LOCATING DUPLICATE FILES

1. Come up with a file name (or partial name) for which you want to search for duplicates. You might do this intuitively. "Hmmm. I *wonder* if there aren't a lot of copies of this Apple Modem Tool lying around in some of my telecom programs," you might think. Or you might think you remember seeing two files with at least similar names. If you have a bunch of free time on your hands, you can even just pick file names from the System Folder in some kind of sequence and check for any or all of them.

2. From the Finder's File menu, choose the Find option.

3. Enter the name or partial name you want to search for.

4. If you're using System 7.1, click on More Choices and then on the All At Once checkbox in the second Find dialog (see Figure 2–9).

Under System 7.5, you don't need to expand the choices offered in the first Find dialog.

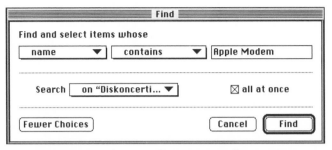

Figure 2–9. Second Find dialog in System 7.1

5. Click on the Find button or press Return.

6. The system will locate all files on all mounted
   hard disks that match the criterion you supplied. Under System 7.5, it will list them in the
   order it locates them in the top pane of the
   Find dialog (see Figure 2–10). You can find out

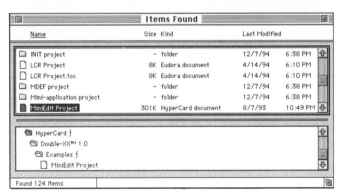

Figure 2–10. Found files dialog in System 7.5

where each is located by clicking on its entry in
the top list. Under System 7.1, after the search
is complete (assuming, of course, that you
asked the system to find all of the occurrences

at once), all of the documents that match the
criterion are highlighted, and the first one is
scrolled into view. You can then scroll around
to find the other documents.

7. You can now look at each of the duplicated
entries and, following the advice above, determine which are candidates for removal from
your hard drive.

---

NOTE: System 7.5 Users Only: If you find
duplicated files and discover that two or
more programs need to use the same
program but expect to find it in different
places, you can take advantage of the
ability to create aliases for files. Just create
an alias of one of the files and then replace
all of the other files with the alias. You can
then delete the duplicated files, and the
applications will work fine.

## WHERE YOU ARE

Now you've really started to hit your stride. You've
really cleaned up your System Folder. If you're typical
of most Mac users I've run into, you've probably
picked up several megabytes of badly needed disk
space by now.

In Chapter 3, we'll tackle the rest of the disk outside your System Folder with the same ruthless vengeance with which we just whittled your System Folder down to a more manageable—and sleeker, more efficient—size.

# CHAPTER 3

## SLIMMING DOWN THE REST OF YOUR DISK

Whew! Aren't you glad you have the messiest part of this System Fitness Plan behind you? Delving into the System Folder and its mysteries should have emboldened you so that you are now ready to try anything.

In this chapter, we'll take a look at some simple exercises you can do involving folders other than the System Folder. Then we'll look at the issue of whether programs that double the amount of space available on your hard disk work well and how you might want to use them. Finally, we'll discuss a disk optimization technique called "defragmentation," which is something like converting fat to muscle instead of eliminating it completely.

### VARIETIES OF DISK BLOAT

Let's start with a little background. Many different kinds of files are candidates for the Disk Bloat reject pile. Here are some of the main kinds of files you might want to delete from your system:

▶ Those you never needed but didn't know were there

▶ Those you needed at one time but probably don't need now

▶ Those you haven't touched since your Aunt
   Tillie got married three years ago and aren't
   likely to touch until her children are in college

▶ Those for which you have an infrequent need
   and that are taking up so much room that they
   ought to become less permanent residents

Files in the first two categories are clear candidates for
removal. Those in the last two categories should probably be archived and then deleted. We'll talk about
archiving files when we consider these types of files.

### STUFF YOU NEVER NEEDED OR DON'T NEED NOW

If you're like most Macintosh owners, you've probably
almost always installed new software using each particular program's easiest (or sometimes even "recom-
mended") installation process. Although 90 percent
of Macintosh programs allow you to choose what is
generally called a "custom" installation rather than
the standard, default installation, you probably don't
use that option.

After all, if the manufacturer of the software has gone
to the trouble of designing a complete installation
program, why should you tinker with it? Simple. It's
your hard disk, not theirs! They couldn't care less how
much stuff you end up with on your disk drive as a
result of their installation. They set up installation
processes that will cause them the minimal number
of headaches and calls for technical support. In the
process, they often put unneeded files into their application folders or into various places in the System
Folder. Chapters 1 and 2 dealt with the system-level

stuff. Let's turn our attention now to the kinds of files that might be lying around your hard disk as a result of full installations of programs.

Many programs install sample, tutorial, or demonstration files as part of their installation process. If you've been using the program for a while, you probably no longer need these files (assuming, of course, that you ever did need them). Let's see how many of these folders and files we can remove from your hard disk.

 ### EXERCISE 14—REMOVING SAMPLES, TUTORIALS, AND DEMONSTRATIONS

1. Repeat Exercise 5, this time concentrating on the folders outside your System Folder. As in Exercise 5, you can probably safely immediately delete these files rather than put them into a holding folder temporarily, since their purpose is clear and no longer appropriate.

2. Now repeat Exercise 5 on the folders outside your System Folder, but this time scan through the folder names for such terms as Demo, Sample, Example, and Tour. Immediately delete any that you clearly don't need.

NOTE: You may want to take the time to scan a printed directory listing of one or more of your application folders that you suspect of containing this type of file. I obviously can't come up with all the possible names software publishers might use to denote a file whose purpose is transitory.

3. Run Exercise 5 one more time, this time looking for a folder name containing the word Template. You'll find that some programs (notably word processors, desktop publishers, and desktop presentation packages) supply you with a sometimes staggering array of templates to use as a starting point for your own projects. Look these over carefully and critically. Do you ever expect, for example, to need to prepare a three-column newsletter? Or a black-and-white Power-Point presentation? Toss those that sound

NOTE: Templates are sometimes stationery documents under System 7. Stationery documents are often treated by their owning applications as if they were locked, but they are not necessarily locked in the Finder. Remember that you can use the Option key to force the Trash to empty even if one or more objects it contains are locked.

unpromising, particularly those connected with
programs you use fairly frequently and for which
you've never needed a particular template.

Another category of files that you probably don't know
exists are temporary files created by applications as a
safeguard against losing data. Sometimes these files
are created in a folder stored in the System Folder, but
often they are created in the application folder.

Most programs are pretty good about cleaning up
after themselves. If they create temporary files while
they are running, they delete those files automatically
when you exit normally. The operative word here,
however, is "normally." If your system crashes or
power goes out while you're in the middle of a session, the applications that are running at the time
never have a chance to do the proper cleanup. As a
result, you can end up with a proliferation of these
temporary files. Many of them take up little space,
but I've seen Word temporary files as big as 500K!
Fortunately, naming conventions make it fairly easy to
locate and delete these temporary files.

 ## EXERCISE 15—REMOVING TEMPORARY FILES

1. Make sure you're not running any applications.
   Some programs create temporary files while
   they are running, if you try to delete them,
   you'll just get frustrated.

**2.** Repeat Exercise 5 on your application folders (at least on those that create documents) and your document folders (where you store documents created by applications that create them). You can probably safely skip telecommunications program folders and games, which seldom create documents, let alone backups of documents. Here are the key search terms:

▶ Temp

▶ Tmp

▶ Bak

▶ Backup

▶ Copy

▶ ~ (tilde)

> NOTE: In case you are terminally curious, the origin of the search term *Bak* goes back to the days of early computers running the CP/M operating system. These systems had what we old-timers sometimes call 8.3 (pronounced "eight dot three") naming conventions. The first part of the file name was limited to eight characters, then a period, followed by the last three characters. Backup files created by almost all programs on such systems were labeled with the Bak three-letter extension. Incidentally, this is the same naming convention followed in MS-DOS (including Microsoft Windows) and PC-DOS. Aren't you glad you're a Macintosh user with file names of thirty-two characters?

### Stale and Seldom-Used Documents

One of the most fruitful areas to search for items to remove from your hard disk is in documents that you created and have since forgotten about. You may or may not feel a need to keep such documents around somewhere, but unless you generally work on projects that span long periods of time, it's probably all right to keep such files archived where you can retrieve them when you need them.

## Archiving Files

Now we'll turn to the topic of archiving files. Then we'll discuss some alternative ways of identifying documents that are candidates for this treatment and how to use archive-and-delete techniques to free up even more Disk Bloat.

### Archiving Techniques

It is probably clear by now that there are two categories of documents on your hard disk: things you put there and things put there by programs you install or use. Items in the first category are safer to delete, because you almost certainly can restore them fairly easily from the disks on which they were originally delivered to you. But before you delete a document you created or obtained from another user, you might well want to make a backup copy of it for safekeeping.

This process of making a backup of a file and then removing it is sometimes called archiving a file. The only trick is remembering where you stored the archive if you need it again after deleting the original

document. You may well want to compress the file as
you archive it so that it takes up less space on the
floppy disk or other medium on which you store it.

You can archive a file to a number of locations. Here
are the most common:

▶ One or more floppy disks or other
  "removable media"

▶ Another hard disk on the same system

▶ A network server disk

▶ An on-line electronic mail or bulletin
  board service

Whichever of these locations you choose, the basic
technique for archiving files remains the same,
as follows:

**1.** Copy the file to the storage location, optionally
   compressing it in the process.

**2.** Delete the original.

**3.** Make a record of where the copy is stored (see
   Exercise 16).

How you retrieve the archived file when you need it
later depends on how you archive it, as you will
soon see.

Whether to compress your files as you archive them is mostly a matter of individual choice. Compressed files take up less space, but when it comes time to retrieve them, you will have to take the time to de-compress (expand) them. If a file is too big to fit on a single floppy disk, you will have to segment it; the capability of doing this is generally part of a compression utility, so you will always have to use a compression program if you need to segment a file.

### FILE-COMPRESSION OPTIONS

Two primary programs are available on the Macintosh for file compression and expansion: StuffIt (which comes in a variety of flavors and versions) and Compact Pro. Which program you use is primarily a matter of personal taste and choice. I prefer Compact Pro, although I use both of these utilities from time to time. My preference is mostly historical, but Compact Pro does seem to create slightly smaller archive files than does StuffIt.

Both of these file-compression utilities can produce two basic types of files: compressed and self-extracting. A compressed file requires the original compression program to be available to decompress it. A self-extracting archive, which is 10–18K larger than the equivalent compressed file, carries along with it the capability of expanding without the original programs being available. You probably don't need to create self-extracting archives, since you will typically be expanding the files yourself on the system on which you compressed them.

NOTE: If you create or download or otherwise obtain self-extracting archives, you may find them taking up a fair amount of space on your hard disk. You can reduce them from self-extracting archives to regular archives with a nifty little freeware program called DeSEA. One of the virtues of this program is that it will work on multiple files without restarting, so you can remove the excess self-extracting code from a collection of self-extracting archives very quickly.

By tradition, compressed files have a file extension associated with them (much as the CP/M and MS-DOS files I talked about earlier had three-character extensions). A compressed archive created with StuffIt, for example, has an extension of "sit"; one created with Compact Pro has an extension of "cpt." Self-extracting archives usually have an extension of "sea," regardless of which program created them. If you had a document called Extraordinary Ideas and you compacted it, its file name would, by default, become one of the following:

▶ Extraordinary Ideas.sit—if you used StuffIt to compress it

▶ Extraordinary Ideas.cpt—if you used Compact Pro to compress it

▶ Extraordinary Ideas.sea—if you created a self-extracting archive using either product

> **NOTE:** Compact Pro is available only as
> shareware. StuffIt Lite is the name of the
> shareware version of the commercial
> product StuffIt Deluxe. You can download
> either or both of these programs from your
> favorite on-line service.

### TRACKING ARCHIVES

If you are a System 7 user, Apple Computer has provided you with a slick way of keeping track of where
your archive files are. If you're a System 6 user, you're
going to have to be a little more creative and do more
of the work yourself, but there are still a couple of
useful techniques for handling this task.

## EQUIPMENT RULE 2—TRACKING ARCHIVES ON SYSTEM 6

1. Locate a document you wish to archive (see Exercise 16).

2. Copy it to its archival destination.

3. Delete it from your hard disk.

4. Create a TeachText document of the same name as the archived document.

5. In the TeachText document, write the location of the archive (for example Floppy disk named

"Archives December 1994"). Now any time you open the document, you'll be told exactly where to find it.

 ## EQUIPMENT RULE 3—TRACKING ARCHIVES ON SYSTEM 7

**1.** Locate a document you wish to archive (see Exercise 16).

**2.** Copy it to its archival destination.

**3.** Delete it from your hard disk.

**4.** Select the archived document in its archived location.

**5.** From the Finder's File menu, choose Make Alias.

**6.** Copy the alias of the archived document to the document's original location on your hard disk.

**7.** Don't forget to delete the alias of the document from the archive location. When you double-click on the alias on your hard disk, the system will prompt you to insert or mount the disk or server on which the archive is located.

## FINDING THE OLD STUFF

Now that we have some basic Equipment Rules for dealing with the archives, how do we locate files that are candidates to be archived?

You'll want to determine your own parameters, depending on how you work, of course. According to the set of rules that I use, I should consider archiving any document that:

▶ hasn't been modified in sixty days and

▶ isn't part of a current project; or

▶ is larger than 100K and hasn't been modified in thirty days.

I don't always *follow* those rules, of course, but those are my guidelines. Locating such documents on your hard disk is pretty easy.

 ## EXERCISE 16—LOCATING OLD FILES

**1.** In the Finder, open the windows and folders in which you wish to search for old documents.

TIP: This is a place where it pays to open folders on the Desktop rather than just expanding their views in the Finder windows.

**2.** From the Finder's View menu, choose By Date.

The files are now sorted so that the longer it's been since you modified them, the lower in the window's scrolling list they will appear.

TIP: In System 7, you can shortcut this menu option by clicking on the label in the Finder window corresponding to the order in which you want to see the files listed. For example, to sort them by their last-modified date, you would just click on Last Modified in the window's header area. Figure 3–1 shows a folder's contents listed in name order. Figure 3–2 shows the same folder in contents order by the date documents were last modified.

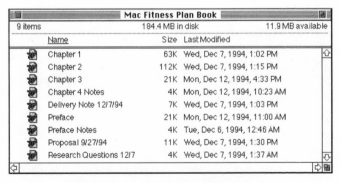

Figure 3–1. Folder sorted by name

| 9 items | | 184.5 MB in disk | 11.9 MB available |
|---|---|---|---|
| | Name | Size | Last Modified |
| 🔧 | Chapter 3 | 21K | Mon, Dec 12, 1994, 4:33 PM |
| 🔧 | Preface | 21K | Mon, Dec 12, 1994, 11:00 AM |
| 🔧 | Chapter 4 Notes | 4K | Mon, Dec 12, 1994, 10:23 AM |
| 🔧 | Proposal 9/27/94 | 11K | Wed, Dec 7, 1994, 1:30 PM |
| 🔧 | Chapter 2 | 112K | Wed, Dec 7, 1994, 1:15 PM |
| 🔧 | Delivery Note 12/7/94 | 7K | Wed, Dec 7, 1994, 1:03 PM |
| 🔧 | Chapter 1 | 63K | Wed, Dec 7, 1994, 1:02 PM |
| 🔧 | Research Questions 12/7 | 4K | Wed, Dec 7, 1994, 1:37 AM |
| 🔧 | Preface Notes | 4K | Tue, Dec 6, 1994, 12:46 AM |

Figure 3–2. Folder sorted by last date modified

NOTE: Since applications don't typically get modified by the user, you'll find that they tend to fall to the bottom of the window when you sort by the last-modified date. That will come in handy as you'll soon see.

## REMOVING APPLICATIONS

In some ways, removing applications is safer than removing documents from your disk. After all, if you delete a program that you later decide you shouldn't have deleted, you can always go back to the original disks and reinstall it. A document you created, though, is a different story; delete one without backing it up or archiving it first, and you could find yourself having to recreate work.

There is one aspect of removing unneeded applications that you should consider carefully before doing. You don't want simply to delete the application file (and, presumably, any supporting documents and files installed in its folder). You also want to remove any vestiges of its existence from your hard disk. In other words, you really want to *uninstall* the application.

Unfortunately, the idea that you might ever want to eradicate from your hard disk any recollection or remnant of a program's existence seldom occurs to the people who write the programs. After all, they see the program they create for you as a masterpiece that you'll never want to do without again in your entire computer life. Only recently has it become considered necessary to include uninstall routines with software, but most commercial programs (as well as virtually all freeware and shareware titles) do not yet incorporate this capability.

As you remove an application from your hard disk, then, you will want to revisit Chapter 2 and some of the earlier exercises in this chapter to assist you in removing other files related to the program you are deleting. This applies particularly to the System Folder, since (presumably, at least) any supporting files installed with the program are either in the application's folder or in the System Folder.

I recommend that you carry out Exercise 17 as a final step after removing any program from your hard disk.

## Exercise 17—Removing All Traces of a Program

(You can do this exercise before removing the application, but it is somewhat cleaner to do so after you believe you've removed all of the program files. You won't run into as many instances of the application's supporting cast this way.)

1. Repeat Exercise 5, focusing on your System Folder. Provide the name of the application (minus any version numbers) as the search term. This will help you uncover Preferences folder entries, startup documents, and folders of supporting resources.

2. Having located any such objects, delete them.

---

There is another way to work with issues of installing and uninstalling software. The disk called *Dr. Dan's Macintosh Fitness Plan Disk*, which you can order by using the form at the back of this book, includes software that will help you keep track of changes made to your disk as a result of installing a program. It generates a log file that you can later use to recover from the installation if you decide to remove the application.

## Doubling Your Disk's Capacity

Several commercial programs that have become available in the past year or two effectively double the amount of information you can store on your hard disk. These seem like magic. (One of my all-time favorite authors, Isaac Asimov, is credited with saying, "Any reasonably interesting technology is indistinguishable from magic.") In practice, how well do they work?

My experience with these programs, both on the Macintosh and on other desktop platforms, has been uniformly good. The programs seem to work reliably, and they clearly do increase disk capacity. They do their work in the background, compressing files that have been identified (by type, not by specific document or object) as acceptable candidates only when your machine isn't working on something more important (which is almost everything). Essentially, these programs compress data just like the programs I mentioned earlier for archiving purposes, but these programs work automatically and in the background rather than in the foreground and only on demand.

If you are running a reasonably fast machine, you won't notice the slowdowns that take place when you ask your system to open a particular document or launch a specific program and that object has been compressed. There is a delay (it would in fact be impossible for there to be no delay, since the decompression clearly introduces a separate step in the launch process), and on older, slower Macintoshes, it can be not only noticeable but also annoying. So if you're still running an old SE/30 or Macintosh II or IIx, you probably don't want to use one of these programs unless it is the last resort and then only until you can afford a faster machine, a bigger hard disk drive, or both.

But if you're running a newer Macintosh with a high-speed CPU, you should definitely consider buying one of the well-known programs for increasing disk capacity. There are several on the market, and differences among them seem to be largely cosmetic, from all I've been able to gather. The best-known products in this category are:

▶ StuffIt SpaceSaver

▶ AutoDoubler

▶ Stacker

▶ TimesTwo

(Actually, Stacker and TimesTwo aren't, strictly speaking, compression programs. They have the same effect as the other programs in this category, but they work differently. Don't worry about understanding how they work, though.)

NOTE: You will probably hear scare stories about people who have lost data—or even entire hard drives of information—because of these programs. I have never seen a

> documented case in which these programs
> could be isolated as being at fault in such
> situations. If you are careful about backing
> up your data, you shouldn't have any
> concern about using these well-
> established programs to give yourself
> greater disk capacity.

You might think that if you use one of these programs,
you can ignore the rest of the advice in this book.
After all, if you can take your 250MB hard disk up
to 500MB (that's a half-gigabyte drive, where *giga*
means *billion*, just in case you want to impress all
of your guests at your next cocktail party), why
would you want to waste time putting it on a
fitness plan?

Wrong! There's a fundamental rule of the universe
that says, "Your need for anything will always expand
to absorb all of the available supply of that something, plus 10 percent." That rule applies to disk drives as well. Trust me. I know.

## WHERE YOU ARE

You've probably recovered several megabytes of Disk
Bloat by now. Your hard disk should be looking and
feeling pretty lean and mean.

In Chapter 4, we're going to do a few simple exercises aimed at improving your system's performance

through making more of its memory (RAM) available.
Although this activity is related only marginally to
Disk Bloat, it is nonetheless helpful. Any good Mac-
intosh needs all the RAM it can get!

# CHAPTER 4

## GIVING YOUR MEMORY SOME ELBOW ROOM

This chapter focuses on making more effective use of the memory (RAM) installed in your Macintosh. Although it is true that short of physically plugging in more RAM chips, you can't do a lot to increase your Macintosh's memory, there are a few exercises you can do that will help you expand available RAM. You can make more memory available by doing any or all of the following (which we'll cover in greater detail in the remainder of the chapter):

▶ Clear out unused or inefficient INITs that load into memory every time you start your system

▶ Change the amount of memory allocated to applications you use frequently

▶ Change your RAM disk and virtual memory settings

▶ Buy software that "tricks" your Macintosh into thinking it has more memory than it really does

### SHEDDING UNSIGHTLY INITS

When your Macintosh starts up, does it seem to you like there are about 100 little icons appearing on the screen? Are you a victim of what has come to be

known as "icon crawl"? If so, you might find yourself
running out of memory more often than you need to.

Most of the icons that appear across the bottom of
your screen as your Macintosh starts up are probably
familiar to you. You probably voluntarily agreed to
have most of them appear there, at some point or
another, whether or not you were aware of the consequences of that decision at the time. Some of those
icons were put there by programs as you installed
them. (Actually, the icons themselves weren't put
there; the icons merely let you know that some system extension is being loaded into memory.)

NOTE: Not all of the system extensions that are
occupying RAM in your Macintosh display
an icon to indicate that they are doing so.
Some such extensions don't have icons;
others allow you to turn their icons on and
off during startup, and you may have elected
at some point not to have them shown.

### WHAT **ARE** THESE THINGS?
INITs are a category of system extension. System extensions, in turn, add functionality to your system
that isn't part of the system software that is always
present. An INIT (the name is taken from the fact that
it is placed into your Macintosh's memory when your
system is being INITialized each time it starts) adds

some capability to your system. You've probably
come to rely on many of these programs. Most of
them are largely transparent.

Control panels are another category of system extension. This type of addition gives you the ability to
control certain aspects of your system by opening a
small window (see Figure 4–1 for an example) and
changing some settings that determine how your
system will behave. Some system extensions have
both an INIT and a control panel, but most come in
one form or the other.

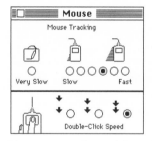

Figure 4–1. Mouse control panel from System 7.x

### How Much Space Do They Occupy?

A good place to start shedding excess RAM weight is
to find out how much of an impact these little critters
have on your system's memory. To do that, you need
to start your Macintosh with no INITs or control panels loaded. Doing that is easy under System 7 and not
so easy under System 6.

EXERCISE 18—DETERMINING IMPACT OF
INITs AND CONTROL PANELS

System 7 Users

**1.** Shut down your Macintosh.

**2.** Start your Macintosh again, but hold down the
Shift key while it starts. Keep holding the Shift
key until you see a message that says "Extensions Off." Then you can release it.

**3.** After your system is fully "awake," choose About
This Macintosh... from the Apple menu (it
should be the first item). You'll see a window
something like the one in Figure 4–2.

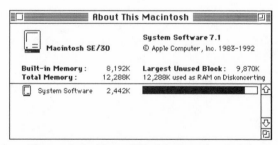

Figure 4–2. About This Macintosh window

**4.** Make a note of how much memory your system
has available.

**5.** Restart your system, this time letting the startup process continue as usual.

6. Once the system is back in operation again, check the amount of memory available.

7. By subtracting the memory available at step 6 from the amount in step 3, you'll be able to find out how much memory the various system extensions your Macintosh uses occupy.

**System 6 Users**

1. From the Apple menu, choose About The Finder.

2. Record the amount of RAM available in your system now, with all of the extensions loaded into memory.

3. Open your System Folder.

4. Create two new folders: Unused Control Panels and Unused INITs.

> **NOTE:** Unlike under System 7, System 6 INITs go by a variety of names and types and are not particularly easy to locate. This, in fact, is one of the biggest improvements from System 6 to System 7 from the standpoint of managing your Macintosh life.

5. From the View menu in the Finder, choose By Kind. This arranges your files by the type of file they are rather than by name or date, as you are

probably accustomed to viewing your files.
(Note that the files are arranged alphabetically
according to their type.)

**6.** Locate the Control Panel files. They will all be
together. Drag them to your newly created Unused Control Panels folder.

**7.** Look for documents that appear to be System
documents. (They have type names like System
Document and Chooser Document.) Locate as
many as you can and drag their icons into the
Unused INITs folder.

**8.** Restart your Macintosh.

**9.** After the system is operational again, check the
memory available, as you did in steps 1 and 2.

**10.** By subtracting the memory available at step 2
from the amount in step 8, you'll be able to find
out how much memory your Macintosh system
extensions occupy.

---

If you think you can gain enough advantage by removing some of the system extensions you don't
need, continue with this section. If the results of
Exercise 18 indicate that your system doesn't have
an excess of system extensions cluttering up memory, skip to the next section, "Reallocating Memory to
Applications."

### Finding and Removing Unneeded Extensions

As was the case with other system documents you ran across in Chapters 1 and 2, you will find that extensions fall into three broad categories: those, like printer drivers, that you recognize and can easily determine whether you need; those, like INITs related to programs you have long since removed, that you can easily determine you don't need; and those about which you haven't the foggiest notion.

By now, you don't need anyone to help you figure out what to do with those INITs and Control Panels that fit into either of the first two categories.

> NOTE: Because the consequences of removing an INIT that your system needs can be fairly painful, I always recommend using the intermediate-folder approach to removing these items. You might create a folder called Extensions (Disabled) and put all INITs in there for several days or weeks before moving them to the Trash. That folder is a place where, unless you are absolutely certain that removing an INIT won't cause a problem, you're better off erring on the side of caution.

Let's see if I can help you figure out how to deal with the INITs and control panels that are mysterious to you. For each unknown extension, perform the steps in Exercise 19 as needed.

### EXERCISE 19—IDENTIFYING UNKNOWN SYSTEM EXTENSIONS

1. Use ResEdit as explained in Chapter 1 to find out what application created the INIT or is associated with it.

2. Compare the Extensions folder with the Control Panels folder to see if a control panel is associated with the INIT. Because control panels have user interfaces associated with them, they usually provide some identifying information that will help you sort out their origin and purpose.

3. Most extensions (INITs) will not respond meaningfully when double-clicked. Usually, the Finder will simply tell you that they can't be opened. Under System 7, the feedback is a bit more informative, but the net result is the same. Still, some extensions do activate. For example, the extension SuperClock!, which is pretty common in the Macintosh community, will open a window that is vaguely reminiscent of a control panel when it's double-clicked. So you might just try double-clicking on a particularly stubborn and obtuse extension. Just don't get your hopes up too high!

4. When all else fails, put the questionable INIT into a holding folder and then restart your system. Use it in the normal way for a few days. If nothing untoward happens, you can probably toss the extension. (Don't forget to back up your System Folder before doing such things, however.)

It is not always necessary or advisable to remove an extension or control panel from your system. Fortunately, there is a somewhat safer way to deal with unknown objects of this type. Apple Computer supplies a control panel called Extensions Manager that can be quite useful when you are dealing with system extensions. (Since Apple distributes this product freely, I've included a copy of it on the *Dr. Dan's Macintosh Fitness Plan Disk* that you can order using the form at the back of this book.) Double-clicking on it brings up a window something like the one in Figure 4–3.

Figure 4–3. Extensions Manager's window

The scrolling list in the Extensions Manager window contains an entry for each extension in your system, whether it is now active or not. Those that are active are highlighted; those that are presently turned off are not highlighted. You can select any extension in this list and turn it on or off. Or you can turn all extensions

on or all extensions off. Next time you restart your
system, extensions will be handled in accordance with
your instructions in this control panel.

Commercial products can provide this same functionality, with additional capabilities. One of the most
popular is NOW Utilities' Startup Manager. With either of these applications—or·something similar—
you can selectively turn extensions on and off and
thus determine what you can safely throw away.

## REALLOCATING MEMORY TO APPLICATIONS

Each application that you run on your Macintosh
occupies a certain amount of memory. The amount it
occupies is determined by the application developer,
but you can change the developer's decision. Sometimes you need to allocate more memory than the
developer thought (perhaps, for example, because
you are working with particularly large and complex
documents or graphics). Sometimes you'll find that
the developer anticipated users doing more complex
things with the program than you need.

Let's take a look at how to find out how much space is
being allocated to your program, how to find out how
much it's actually using, and how to adjust memory
allocation as appropriate.

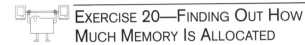 Exercise 20—Finding Out How
Much Memory Is Allocated

**1.** Select an application icon in the Finder.

**2.** From the File menu, choose Get Info or press
Command-I. A window something like the one
in Figure 4–4 opens.

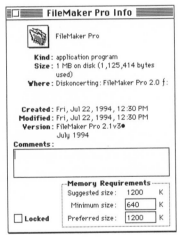

Figure 4–4. Typical Get Info window

**3.** Note the three numbers in the lower-right corner of this window. (If you are running System
6, you'll see only two numbers: one for the suggested size and one for the preferred size. The
principles in this exercise are nonetheless useful and valid.) Two of these numbers are ed-
itable, as indicated by the fact that they are
inside rectangles. We'll come back to editing
these values in Exercise 22.

**4.** As you can see in Figure 4–4, FileMaker Pro on my system is set up so that it prefers 1200K (or 1.2MB) of memory available but will open if as little as 640K is available. For each application whose memory allocation you wish to examine, make a note of these two values. The suggested size is proposed by the developer.

When you launch an application, the system allocates memory using roughly the following scheme:

**1.** If the amount of memory indicated as its Pre-ferred size is available, it allocates that much space.

**2.** If the amount of memory indicated as its Pre-ferred size is not available, it looks at the Mini-mum size. If that amount of memory is available, it allocates that much space. If more than the Minimum but less than the Preferred size is available, it allocates all available memory.

**3.** If the Minimum size amount of memory isn't available, the system refuses to launch the pro-gram and notifies you that insufficient memory is available. (Under System 7, it also suggests ways to solve the problem. For example, if it notices that an application is running with no windows open, it might suggest closing that program to free up memory.)

Just because your system allocates a certain amount of memory to an application doesn't mean that the application is using all of the allocated space. When releasing a program, the developer decides how much space to request, based on testing, what typical users will likely want to do, and so forth. Your mileage may vary, so you may need or wish to "tweak" memory allocation from time to time.

Under System 7 (if you're a System 6 user, you can skip to the end of Exercise 21 now), you can find out exactly how much space a program is using at any moment. This is a little-known feature of System 7.

### Exercise 21—Finding Out How Much Memory a System 7 Program Is Using

1. Open one or more of your favorite applications. If you like, open a document or two (or several) so that you are in a typical usage situation with each application.

2. Return to the Finder by selecting it from the Application menu at the upper-right corner of the screen.

3. From the Apple menu, choose About This Macintosh. You'll see the expected window, with each active application shown. Note that each application has a bar graph associated with it. The filled-in portion of this bar indicates what

portion of the total allocated memory (represented by the entire bar) the application is now using.

**4.** Now comes the neat part. From the Balloon help menu just to the left of the Application menu in the upper-right portion of your screen, choose Show Balloons.

**5.** Now point at the bar associated with any active program. A balloon appears telling you exactly how much memory the program is allocated and exactly how much it is now using.

**6.** Now compare the amount of space the application is using with the amounts allocated and minimum size you found in Exercise 20. Note which applications have more space allocated than you seem to need.

Once you've found a program that seems to have more space available than it really needs for you, you can free up memory by reallocating its space.

### EXERCISE 22—REALLOCATING MEMORY TO A PROGRAM

**1.** Select the program's icon in the Finder.

**2.** From the File menu, choose Get Info or press Command-I.

**3.** In the resulting dialog box, change the preferred size value to a more reasonable number, based on your findings in Exercise 20 (if you're a System 7 user) or on your intuitive feeling about how much program space you actually need (if you're a System 6 user). You'll find that you cannot set the Preferred size smaller than the Minimum size. An attempt to do so produces a dialog like the one shown in Figure 4–5.

Figure 4–5. Notification of attempt to set Preferred size too low

NOTE: I recommend that you never change the Minimum size unless you find it absolutely necessary. Nasty crashes can result from setting this value too low.

## CHANGING DISK CACHE AND VIRTUAL MEMORY SETTINGS

Under both Systems 6 and 7, you can allocate space to what is called a disk cache. Under System 7, you can set up space on your hard disk to be treated as if it were memory, a scheme called virtual memory. In this section, we'll take a look at these two capabilities and how they affect RAM and disk space availability on your system.

### YOU CAN'T SPEND DISK CACHE

A disk cache is a portion of your computer's memory that is set aside for the system to use. It uses this area of memory in ways designed to accelerate performance.

In the absence of such a cache, certain kinds of information your programs use can be "purged" from memory while the program is running. (This process is perfectly safe and an entirely appropriate design decision made by the developer of the program in question. The information isn't lost; it is simply removed from memory until needed again, generally to make way for something the program considers more currently important or useful.) For example, if you are using a word processor and you ask it to find a phrase in your document, the program code and the dialog box that assist in that process are both loaded into your program's portion of the Macintosh's memory. When the find operation completes, the word processor might decide it needs more space for more text or a font change. In that case, it unloads, or purges, the find-related objects from its memory space. These objects remain on your disk, of course, and can be easily retrieved by the program when they are needed again.

A disk cache acts as a kind of halfway house for this kind of information. If you have a disk cache turned on (under System 7, it is always turned on) and it is large enough to be helpful, the system routes purged objects to the disk cache area of memory rather than simply removing them. The net effect is that if you suddenly need one of the objects stored in the disk cache portion of RAM, retrieving it is significantly faster than reading it from your disk drive. Thus frequently used items are more immediately available to your program.

The problem, of course, is that the area of RAM set aside as a disk cache isn't accessible to your programs for any use that the system doesn't intend. If you have a large disk cache, you are depriving your applications of space. Make the disk cache big enough, and you may find yourself unable to load as many programs as you'd like.

### Exercise 23—Adjusting Your Disk Cache on System 7

1. In your Control Panels folder, inside your System Folder, you'll find a control panel called Memory. Double-click on it. The resulting window in System 7 looks like Figure 4–6. (It is considerably different under System 6 because System 6 doesn't support virtual memory or 32-bit addressing, but the disk cache principles are the same on both versions of the system.) PowerBook systems—and some desktop Macintosh models—also have an additional capability to create a RAM disk. I won't cover RAM disks in this book except to say that they are operationally quite similar to disk caches.

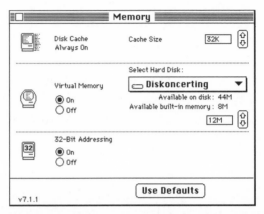

Figure 4–6. Memory control panel (System 7)

**2.** If you are using System 6, determine whether
the Disk Cache is enabled. If it isn't, you may
want to turn it on and set its size in accordance
with the advice in this exercise. If you try that for
a while and find it doesn't noticeably increase
performance, you can always turn it off.

**3.** Note how much RAM is devoted to the disk
cache. The minimum cache size is 32K. The
maximum size of the cache available is 2560K
(2.5MB). Unless you change it, your disk cache
will probably be 256K.

**4.** Decide what size disk cache you want to use.
(See the discussion immediately following this
exercise for some guidelines.)

**5.** Use the up and down arrows next to the cache
size indicator to change the size of the cache
accordingly.

**6.** Close the Memory control panel and reset your machine so the changes will take effect.

---

## SETTING YOUR DISK CACHE SIZE

How do you decide what size disk cache will work best for you? Unfortunately, there's no useful formula that will work for all cases; trial and error will determine its optimal setting for you. However, I can offer some guidelines based on experience.

If you frequently run out of memory when you try to load an application or open a large document and your Macintosh has at least 8MB of RAM (under System 7) or 4MB of RAM (under System 6), you probably want to keep the disk cache off (under System 6) or at 32K (under either System 6 or System 7).

If you have a lot of memory (more than 8MB) and a relatively slow machine (one with less than a 68040 microprocessor in it), consider boosting the disk cache as high as it will go. Then back it off if you run into out-of-memory problems later.

If you are the kind of user who typically has only one or two applications open at a time and you have more than 8MB of RAM, you'll almost certainly notice significant performance increases by opening up a maximum disk cache.

In all likelihood, you fall somewhere between these guidelines, so you'll have to fall back on my first bit of advice: Try different settings and find one that gives you a good balance of performance versus out-of-memory conditions.

NOTE: How do you find out whether you have a slower microprocessor in your system? Probably the easiest way is to ask your dealer or someone who knows the Macintosh product line. If that's not possible (or you're not comfortable asking), you can obtain About This Macintosh or a similar program from your favorite on-line service. (The program also appears on the disk you can order from me with the form at the back of this book.) When you run that program, it produces a window like the one shown in Figure 4–7.

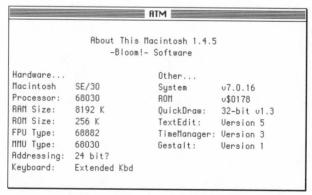

```
                          ATM

                   About This Macintosh 1.4.5
                      -Bloom!- Software

Hardware...                   Other...
Macintosh    SE/30            System        v7.0.16
Processor:   68030            ROM           v$0178
RAM Size:    8192 K           QuickDraw:    32-bit v1.3
ROM Size:    256 K            TextEdit:     Version 5
FPU Type:    68882            TimeManager:  Version 3
MMU Type:    68030            Gestalt:      Version 1
Addressing:  24 bit?
Keyboard:    Extended Kbd
```

Figure 4–7. About This Macintosh program window

If the processor is not a 68040 (or at least a 68030), you can conclude that you are running a relatively slow Processor. (The key number is the second from the end.)

If instead of a number that looks like 680X0, where X is some number, you see a shorter number, possibly preceded by the letters PPC, you are running a Power-Mac, and you can forget about slow processors!

### VIRTUAL MEMORY

Beginning with System 7, Apple Computer made it possible to expand the amount of memory your Macintosh *thinks* it has by setting aside virtual memory space on your hard disk. This space is treated for most purposes exactly as if it were RAM.

Virtual memory is a two-edged sword. On the one hand, it can make a system with relatively little RAM far more usable by giving it more memory capacity. On the other hand, it occupies a potentially significant percentage of your hard disk drive space. Ultimately you must decide on the trade-off between virtual memory and free disk space. The more RAM you have, the less likely you are to benefit from virtual memory.

The amount of virtual memory you can allocate depends on your hard disk capacity and the amount of physical RAM your Macintosh has. The Memory control panel (which we saw in Figure 4–7) has a place for you to determine how much virtual memory to allocate. Although it is possible to allocate all of your available disk space (which is shown in the Memory control panel), in practice you will probably never do that. Experience seems to indicate that a virtual memory setting larger than 1.5 times your total physical RAM is probably not going to be used very efficiently (for lots of technical reasons that are well beyond the scope of this book). At most, I recommend allocating twice the virtual memory as you have RAM.

If you have a system with 32MB of RAM, virtual memory is probably not an important consideration. You can probably do quite well with the physical RAM available.

## Tricking Your Mac's Memory

If you really need more RAM and none of the tricks and exercises in this chapter help enough, you can buy a commercial software product called RAM Doubler and effectively (as its name promises) double the amount of RAM in your system. This means that if you have an 8MB Macintosh, you can turn it instantly and magically into a 16MB machine, for a cost of less than $100 at this writing.

There will undoubtedly be other programs like RAM Doubler on the market, probably by the time you read this. User experience with RAM Doubler indicates that it is quite safe and effective. At today's memory chip prices, it's also a bargain.

## WHERE YOU ARE

Well, by now you should have a pretty lean Macintosh working for you. You should be making maximum use of both disk space and memory.

In Chapter 5, we'll take a look at some techniques for keeping things from running to flab ever again.

# CHAPTER 5

## KEEPING YOUR MACINTOSH IN SHAPE

This is our cool-down chapter. Now that you have your Macintosh running lean and mean, this chapter offers a few simple tips and techniques you can use to keep things from getting out of hand.

I'll discuss the following topics in this final chapter:

▶ Organizing your hard disk for better maintenance

▶ Monitoring disk utilization

▶ Tracking application and document usage

▶ Tracking installation changes

▶ Miscellaneous tips and hints

### ORGANIZING YOUR HARD DISK

Macintosh users generally put together three basic organizational schemes consciously. (There are also lots of Macintosh users whose "organizational scheme" is more like "put things wherever they land." I won't discuss that approach here, for reasons I hope are obvious!)

First, some users organize all their files functionally.
Each application is in its own folder. Each project or
product or business purpose is in its own folder.
Sometimes folders are grouped. For example, such a
person might have a folder called Projects, inside of
which each project has its own folder. I'll call these
people Functional Organizers (without meaning to
imply anything about their psychological profile).

Second, some users organize their files by type. They
have a folder called Applications, in which each application has its own folder. They have a folder called
Documents in which each document type (or collection of similar documents) has its own folder. These
people will be called Type Organizers.

Finally, some people organize their files by application.
They have a folder called, for example, WordPerfect, in
which they store all of the WordPerfect documents they
create. They might create folders inside that folder so
that documents of a particular type end up filed together. I'll call these people Application Organizers.

I find Functional Organizers to be the most efficient
in terms of their disk usage. Because they organize
their files functionally, they can easily archive, delete,
and otherwise manage groups of files that pertain to
a particular project, task, or activity. When the specific
task is completed, they don't have to hunt all over
their hard disks; they simply archive and delete a single folder and get on with their lives.

Type Organizers have the advantage of always knowing
what application works with a particular document.

If they think of their systems in terms of the programs they run, they probably have an easier time finding a specific file. But archiving and deleting are sometimes challenging, because without a second layer of organization, identifying the files to store may not be very easy or obvious.

Application Organizers seem to me to have the biggest problem with disk organization. If you are working on a project that generates fifteen memos, three letters, twelve reports, five spreadsheets, two databases, and a couple hundred slide presentations, you're going to have a difficult time finding all of the documents related to the project when it expires or goes into retirement.

## Monitoring Disk Usage

It would be useful to develop a new habit of checking periodically to see how much of your hard disk space is available. When you see it approaching the point where 10 percent or less of its space will be free, you can start to work on disk maintenance, using the techniques in Chapters 1–4 before you find yourself in a tight corner.

If you're a System 6 user, you will need to know how much total capacity your hard disk has; the system won't give you this information. If, however, you are using System 7, you can ask the Finder to tell you how much total disk space a particular drive has and how much of that space is available.

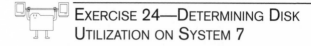

## EXERCISE 24—DETERMINING DISK UTILIZATION ON SYSTEM 7

1. Open the Views control panel. The resulting window should look like Figure 5–1.

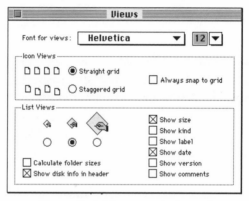

Figure 5–1. Views control panel

2. Make sure the checkbox labeled Show disk info in header is checked.

3. Now all of your Finder windows will display information in their headers about the size of the hard disk on which they are located and how much of that disk is available for use.

4. If you get into the habit of looking at the folder headers periodically, you'll quickly develop a relatively painless way to monitor disk activity.

If you're the absentminded type or just don't want to be bothered with this problem, you can use the Space Monitor program on *Dr. Dan's Macintosh Fitness Plan Disk*, which you can order using the form at the back of this book. This program looks at your disk space situation on all mounted drives each time you start your Macintosh and politely suggests that you clear some space when it detects a potential or upcoming problem.

## WHAT DO YOU USE MOST OFTEN?

Several times, particularly in Chapters 1 and 2, I have suggested that you keep track of which applications and documents you use most often. If your life isn't too complicated, this may be something you can easily do mentally. If that's not easy, keeping notes about your activities (a good idea in any case) either in a text document on your system or on paper may be helpful.

But if your life is complex and you do lots of tasks with different applications and documents, you might benefit from obtaining a copy of TimeLog from Coral Research. This program keeps track of the applications and documents you have open and active as you work. It will produce textual and graphical reports tracking your activity.

However you do it, keeping records like these will help you decide quickly what to archive or delete when the time comes to slim your hard disk drive.

## TRACKING INSTALLATION CHANGES

The good news is that installing Macintosh software is about as automatic a process as you're likely to find. The bad news is that it's so automatic that it goes on largely behind your back, sometimes with unfortunate side effects. One of those side effects, as you saw while doing the exercises in Chapters 1–3, is that files you will never need end up bloating your hard disk. Unfortunately, the Macintosh world hasn't yet caught up with the need for a full-blown, standardized way of keeping track of what is installed where by each program's installation process.

I provide a modest step in that direction with the Deinstaller program on *Dr. Dan's Macintosh Fitness Plan Disk*. This utility isn't nearly as automatic as a full-blown commercial program should be, but it is useful nonetheless. You run Deinstaller just before and immediately following an installation of software on your system. The program creates a file called Deinstall Program (substituting the name of the program you've installed for the word Program as it does). Then if you decide to deinstall the program, you just double-click on that file, and Deinstaller takes care of removing every vestige it can find of the program and related documents.

Short of that, you can always just print the contents of your System Folder before and after an installation and note differences. Keep these printouts in a notebook for easy retrieval later, and you can greatly simplify your life as a Macintosh power user.

## MISCELLANEOUS TIPS AND HINTS

Some stuff just doesn't fit anywhere. That's the point of this concluding section in our cool-down exercise routine. Things aren't in any particular order here, other than the order they happened to occur to me. I hope you'll find a gem or two.

Once a month, set aside an hour or two to do serious hard disk maintenance. During this session, you should:

▶ Perform a full backup of your hard disk (or an incremental backup if you are accustomed to using that approach).

▶ Archive and delete (or alias) old files.

▶ Seriously consider each application on your disk, asking yourself if it's useful enough to justify the amount of space it occupies.

▶ Run a disk optimizer to defragment your drive as described in Chapter 3.

Get into the habit of deleting archived and self-extracting archive files you obtain from others and from on-line services as soon as you have verified that their contents have extracted correctly. Particularly if you are active in an on-line service, these archives can accumulate multiple megabytes of data that is all but transparent to you without a thorough search of your disk.

Use aliases to create the illusion of a document's being stored in more than one place. If you organize your disk functionally, for example, but you have a status report that covers three projects, put it into one of those projects' folder and then put aliases of it into the other project folders. Each alias takes up only 4K of disk space. This is vastly preferable to storing multiple copies of the document. (System 6 users won't be able to use aliases, but you can use the trick I describe in Chapter 3 in the archiving discussion and create a document of the same name whose contents simply tell you where to find the real document.)

If you're still running System 6, switch to System 7.1. I'm not sure most people yet need to move to System 7.5, which occupies considerably more RAM than 7.1, but System 7 has enough advantages over System 6 that you should definitely move to it if you can.

# COMMON MACINTOSH FILE CREATORS AND TYPES

The tables that make up the bulk of this appendix list the most common Macintosh programs, along with their creator codes and file types. These pieces of information, used with ResEdit as described in Chapter 1 and elsewhere in this book, will enable you to identify "orphaned" files on your hard disk and more correctly determine whether they should be deleted.

Table A–1 is sorted in creator code order. Table A–2 is sorted by application name. Most of the time when you use ResEdit, knowing the creator code is sufficient, but as you will see in the tables, some applications create multiple types of files. It may be useful to know not only the application that created the file but also the type of file.

I owe Bob Pratt, retired engineer and Boston Computer Society member extraordinaire, a big vote of thanks. Bob has made a hobby of collecting these creator codes for many years and supplied the vast majority of those presented in these tables.

## TABLE A–1. CREATOR CODES FOR COMMON APPLICATIONS, SORTED BY CREATOR CODE

| CREATOR CODE | PROGRAM NAME—FILE TYPE | FILE TYPE |
|---|---|---|
| 1Aid | 1st Aid - Recovered Fragment | FRAG |
| 1Aid | 1st Aid - Recovered File | GOOD |
| 1Aid | 1st Aid - Extracted Text | TEXT |
| 2CTY | PublishIt! Easy - Input Filter | ROFT |
| 2CTY | PublishIt! Easy - Help | SHLP |
| 2CTY | PublishIt! Easy - Hyphenation | SHYP |
| 2CTY | PublishIt! Easy - Layouts | SPUC |
| 2CTY | PublishIt! Easy - Document | SPVB |
| 2CTY | PublishIt! Easy - Dictionary | SSPL |
| 2CTY | PublishIt! Easy - data | TEXT |
| 4D02 | 4th Dimension - Project | BAS2 |
| 4D02 | 4th Dimension - data | data |
| 4D02 | 4th Dimension - Flag | FLAG |
| 4D02 | 4th Dimension - Index | INDX |
| 4DO3 | 4th Dimension 2.0 - data | 4DES |
| 4DO3 | 4th Dimension 2.0 - Templates | 4DET |
| ???? | Auto Doubler - Re BNDLer | APPL |
| ???? | Freedom of the Press - Installer | APPL |
| ???? | Apple File Exchange - BCS.RTF | TEST |
| ???? | PageMaker 5.0 - Templates | TEXT |
| ???? | Quicken - Home Categories | TEXT |
| Aard | InitPicker - Sound | IPsn |
| aca3 | FreeHand - data | acf3 |
| aCf2 | DeltaGraph - Delta Sim | LWFN |
| AcPC | Access PC - data | APCd |
| ACTA | Acta file | OTLN |
| adbk | Address List | adli |
| ADrk | After Dark - files | ADgm |
| AGXS | Astound - to AGX-Mac | APPL |
| ALD4 | PageMaker 4.0 - Ald Eng | ALC4 |
| ALD4 | PageMaker 4.2 - Additions | ALD4 |
| ALD4 | PageMaker 4.0 - Prep | ALDP |
| ALD4 | PageMaker 4.0 - Kern Tracks | ALQ4 |
| ALD4 | PageMaker 4.2 - Resources | ALR4 |
| ALD4 | PageMaker 4.2 - Dictionary Editor | AMD4 |
| ALD4 | PageMaker 4.2 - Dictionary | AND4 |
| ALD4 | PageMaker 4.0 - Colors | BClf |

| CREATOR CODE | PROGRAM NAME—FILE TYPE | FILE TYPE |
|---|---|---|
| ALD4 | PageMaker 4.2 - Filters | FCD4 |
| ALD4 | Nisus 3.04 - Import | FCOD |
| ALD4 | PageMaker 4.0 - Filters | FCOD |
| ALD4 | PageMaker 4.2 - Help | PRH1 |
| ALD5 | PageMaker 5.0 - Additions | ALD5 |
| ALD5 | PageMaker 5.0 - Other Stuff | ALD5 |
| ALD5 | PageMaker 5.0 - PM5 Defaults | ALF5 |
| ALD5 | PageMaker 5.0 - Color | BClf |
| ALD5 | PageMaker 5.0 - Filter | FLT3 |
| ALD5 | PageMaker 5.0 - Help | PRH1 |
| ALZI | Digital Darkroom - data | ACMP |
| ALZI | Digital Darkroom | ALZC |
| ALZI | Digital Darkroom - Installer | APPL |
| AOp2 | Darwin's Dilemma - Sample | DDGM |
| AOp2 | Darwin's Dilemma - Standard | DDST |
| Arfz | StuffIt Deluxe 3.0 - Unstuffit | APPL |
| ARQM | Morph - data | MORF |
| ARQM | Morph - Photo | MORF |
| ASBM | dBase Mac | ADBE |
| ASPF | Adobe Type Mgr. - Fonts | LWFN |
| ASPL | Astound - Player | APPL |
| atdv | AppleTalk Remote - Network | cdev |
| ATMC | Adobe Type Manager - ATM 68000 | ATMD |
| ATR | Adobe Type Manager - Type Reunion | INIT |
| AUSt | StuffIt Deluxe 2.0 - Self Unstuffer | SIT! |
| aust | FirstClass - Settings | APPL |
| BARC | Frontier - Bar Chart | APPL |
| BAT | MacProject II - FM Export Data | TEXT |
| bbkr | QuicKeys 2 - Installer | APPL |
| BBSR | 1st Desk - Settings | BBSR |
| bjbc | AppleTalk Remote - Script | bjbc |
| BnHg | FirstClass - Bin Hex | APPL |
| BnHq | Binhex - data | TEXT |
| BOBO | ClarisWorks 2 - data Data Base | CWDB |
| BOBO | ClarisWorks 2 - data Word | CWGR |
| BOBO | ClarisWorks 2 - data Spreadsheet | CWSS |
| BOBO | ClarisWorks 2 - Color Gradient | dCol |
| BOBO | ClarisWorks 2 - Name & Address | sWDB |
| BOBO | ClarisWorks 2 - Stationery | sWWP |
| bpas | Sound Edit Pro - Serial Sw. | cdev |
| BRID | SuperCard - Bridge | APPL |
| BWks | WordPerfect Works - Database | BWdb |
| BWks | WordPerfect Works - Draw | BWdr |

| Creator Code | Program Name—File Type | File Type |
|---|---|---|
| BWks | WordPerfect Works - Paint | BWpt |
| BWks | WordPerfect Works - Spreadsheet | BWss |
| BWks | WordPerfect Works - WP | BWwp |
| C*SS | Now Up-to-Date - Server | INIT |
| Cal* | Now Up-to-Date - Calendar | C*DB |
| Cal* | Now Up-to-Date - Appointment Book | C*DR |
| CCMa | Carbon Copy Mac - Help | CCHP |
| CCMa | Carbon Copy Mac - Serial Setup | PORT |
| CdMn | Talking Moose - Phrases | MOOP |
| CDpf | MacWrite II - Dictionary | CMdt |
| CDpf | MacWrite II - Dictionary, UK | CMut |
| CEBN | Calendar Maker - Paint | PNTG |
| CECM | Calendar Maker - Icon Mover | APPL |
| CEDA | QuickMail Remote - Help | QMHP |
| CEIM | Calendar Maker - Icons | CEIF |
| CEKM | QuicKeys 2 - Dialog Keys | cdev |
| CELD | DiskTop - Init | INIT |
| CELM | QuickMail - Resources | CCde |
| CELM | QuickMail - Help | QMHP |
| CEtb | DiskTop - CE TB Preferences | DATA |
| CEtb | CE Toolbox | INIT |
| CEtb | DiskTop - CE Toolbox | INIT |
| CEtb | QuicKeys 2 - Tool Box | INIT |
| CGMK | Common Ground - Auto Maker | APPL |
| CGMK | Common Ground - CG Maker | APPL |
| CGMK | Common Ground | PREF |
| CGRF | Cricket Graph - data | CGTX |
| ClnH | MacWrite II - Claris Help | HCOD |
| ClrH | FileMaker Pro - Claris Help | HCOD |
| ClrH | MacWrite Pro - Claris Help System | HCOD |
| Clro | In Control - Extend | CLRS |
| Clro | In Control - Translators | Fltr |
| Clrs | ClarisWorks 2 - Extend | CLRS |
| CMC | Color MacCheese - Preferences | CMCπ |
| CMC | Color MacCheese - data | PICT |
| cnbf | VersaTerm-PRO - FTM Tools | fbnd |
| CPC* | Compact Pro - Archive | PACT |
| CrCr | ClickPaste - Object | CpCf |
| CRGR | Cricket Graph III - data data | CGDW |
| CRGR | Cricket Graph III - data Graph | CGGW |
| CRGR | Cricket Graph III - Preferences | CGPR |
| CRGR | Cricket Graph III - Palettes | CPAL |
| CRGR | Cricket Graph III - data | CRGF |

| CREATOR CODE | PROGRAM NAME—FILE TYPE | FILE TYPE |
|---|---|---|
| CRGR | Cricket Graph III - Help | HELP |
| CRPR | Cricket Presents - data | CRTM |
| CSpf | MacWrite Pro - Main Dictionary | CMdp |
| CSpf | FileMaker Pro - Dictionary | CMdt |
| CSpf | FileMaker Pro 2.0 - User Dictionary | CUdt |
| CSpf | MacWrite Pro - User Dictionary | CUdt |
| CSpt | ClarisWorks 2 - Dictionary (User) | CUdt |
| CSpt | ClarisWorks 2 - Dictionary (Main) | QMdt |
| CxPB | QuicKeys 2 - Power Book | QKex |
| DACL | DAC Easy Light - data | CHRT |
| DACL | DAC Easy Light - Help | DHlp |
| DAD2 | Canvas - Help | BIFF |
| DAD2 | Canvas - Dictionary | CONF |
| DAD2 | Canvas - Preferences | def2 |
| DAD2 | Canvas - data | drw2 |
| DAD2 | Canvas - Color Tables | drwC |
| DAD2 | Canvas - Macro | Ma3R |
| DAMV | DA Mover - data | DESK |
| DAS | Dollars & Sense - data | DASD |
| dbIN | DateBook - Icon Library | INIT |
| DDAP | Auto Doubler - data | ADDA |
| DDAP | Auto Doubler - Expand | APPL |
| DDRP | Auto Doubler - Verify/Rep | APPL |
| DECO | Cricket Color Paint - data | CRCP |
| DFBO | MicroPhone - data | DFBA |
| DFBO | MicroPhone II - Modem | DFBB |
| DGRH | DeltaGraph Pro - Dictionary | DGmD |
| DGRH | DeltaGraph Pro - Stationery | DGPD |
| DGRH | DeltaGraph - 3D Perspective | DGRD |
| DGRH | DeltaGraph Pro - User Dictionary | DGuD |
| DGRH | DeltaGraph Pro - Tutorial | DSPF |
| DGRH | DeltaGraph - Help | HELP |
| DGRH | DeltaGraph Pro - Library | LBR2 |
| DGRH | DeltaGraph - Library | LIBR |
| DGRH | DeltaGraph - Preferences | PREF |
| DGRH | DeltaGraph - Color | SPID |
| DIDR | Digital Darkroom - Drawings | DIDA |
| dkpt | DiskTop - Preferences | Pfef |
| DkTP | DiskTop - Extras | INIT |
| DmEa | QuicKeys 2 - Dis. Mounty | QKex |
| DMOV | Daymaker - Alarm | DFIL |
| DMOV | Dynodex - DA | DFIL |
| DMOV | InTouch - DA | DFIL |

| CREATOR CODE | PROGRAM NAME—FILE TYPE | FILE TYPE |
|---|---|---|
| DMOV | InTouch - Network - DA | DFIL |
| DMOV | Norton Utilities 2.0 - Fast Find | DFIL |
| DMOV | OnLocation - DA | DFIL |
| dMRN | Now Utilities - SB Preferences | dMDT |
| dMRN | Now Utilities - SB Extra | ECR1 |
| DnPg | Dynodex - Control Panel | cdev |
| DnPg | Dynodex - Paper | VLnf |
| DOCS | Frontier - Data Base | DBAS |
| Dpnt | DeskPaint - Color | Dpol |
| Dpnt | DeskPaint - data | PNTG |
| Dpnt | DeskPaint - Help | ZHLP |
| dPro | MacDraw Pro - Pantone Palettes | dCol |
| dPro | MacDraw Pro - data | dDoc |
| dPro | MacDraw Pro - Slides | dLib |
| dPro | MacDraw Pro - Stationery | dSta |
| DSAT | SAT - Celina V1 | SATT |
| DtBk | DateBook - Preferences | PREF |
| dTbk | Cricket Data III - data | dbTX |
| DTRS | Auto Doubler - Desk Top Reset | APPL |
| DVDT | Apple File Exchange - DT Translation | MLSD |
| DVPC | Lap Link Plus PC - Cable to Pc | MLSD |
| DVUE | OverVUE - Formatted Data | DVSH |
| DVUE | OverVUE - Text data | TEXT |
| DYNO | Dynodex - Day Timer | DYAD |
| DYNO | Dynodex - Time Design | DYAD |
| DYNO | Dynodex - data | DYDB |
| DYNO | Dynodex - Apple Image | DYED |
| DYNO | Dynodex 3.0 - Co Star Layout | DYEN |
| DYNO | Dynodex - Help | DYHP |
| DYNO | Dynodex - Paper Direct | DYLB |
| DYNO | Dynodex 3.0 - Address Change | DYMM |
| DYNO | Dynodex - Portfolio | JNPD |
| ec12 | Can Opener - State | caoS |
| ec12 | Can Opener - Library | oLIB |
| EDIT | Freedom of the Press - Configure | TEXT |
| EEfi | Easy Envelopes | rsrc |
| eeTB | QuicKeys 2 - Configure TB | APPL |
| EGAP | Dollars & Sense 4.1 - data | EGAD |
| EGAP | Dollars & Sense 4.1 - Help | EGAH |
| ENV5 | Mac Envelope - Templates | ENDF |
| ENV5 | Mac Envelope - Lists | EV4Z |
| et20 | AppleTalk Remote - EtherNet 2 | cdev |
| FOXX | FoxPro 2.5 - Data Base File | F+DB |

| CREATOR CODE | PROGRAM NAME—FILE TYPE | FILE TYPE |
|---|---|---|
| FOXX | FoxPro 2.5 - Index File | FCDX |
| FOXX | FoxPro 2.5 - Program File | F+PR |
| FOXX | FoxPro 2.5 - Form File | F+DT |
| Famx | Adobe Type Manager | APPL |
| FCui | FirstClass - Local | FCsf |
| FCui | FirstClass - Phone Book | FCsf |
| FILE | MS File - Help | FHLP |
| FILE | MS File - Form | FORM |
| FILE | MS File - Formatted Data | ISAM |
| flip | In Control - data | FLIP |
| flip | In Control - Samples | FLIP |
| fmcc | Frontier - Preferences | FMPR |
| fmcc | Frontier - Finder Menu | INIT |
| FMKR | FileMaker Plus - data | FMKD |
| FMPR | FileMaker Pro - Template | FMPR |
| FMPR | FileMaker Pro 2.0 - Data | FMPR |
| FMPR | FileMaker Pro 2.0 - Events | FMPR |
| FMPR | FileMaker Pro - Help | STAX |
| Fram | FrameMaker - Help | FHlp |
| Fram | FrameMaker - Dictionary | FUdc |
| FRCS | Freedom of the Press 4.0 - Metrics | FPDF |
| FRCS | Freedom of the Press - Outline | FPDR |
| FRCS | Freedom of the Press - Language | FPER |
| FRDP | Freedom of the Press - Spooler 1.1 | APPL |
| FRPS | Freedom of the Press - Spooler 1.2 | APPL |
| FSPE | DesignStudio - Riff | RIFF |
| FSSC | Sound Play - data | FSSD |
| FWRT | Full Write Prof. - Dictionary | FWDI |
| FWRT | Full Write Prof. - Glossary | FWGL |
| FWRT | Full Write Prof. - data | FWRT |
| FWRT | Full Write Prof. - Stationery | FWST |
| FWRT | Full Write Prof. - Thesaurus | FWTI |
| FWRT | Full Write Prof. - User Dictionary | FWUD |
| GAnt | MacSchedule - data | EASy |
| GDEX | TouchBase - data | GDEX |
| GDG2 | QuicKeys 2 - Template Printer | APPL |
| GDPS | Astound - English Dict. | GDIC |
| GEOL | AppleLink - Help | HLPF |
| GEOL | AppleLink - CCL | PETE |
| GEOL | AppleLink - Resources | rsrc |
| GLAS | Full Impact - data | ADGH |
| GLAS | Full Impact - Macros | GMAC |
| Heap | QuicKeys 2 - Heap Framer | APPL |

| CREATOR CODE | PROGRAM NAME—FILE TYPE | FILE TYPE |
|---|---|---|
| HELX | Helix - Formatted Data | HEAP |
| HELX | Helix, Double - data | HEAP |
| HELX | Helix - Help | HEXT |
| HELX | Helix - Text Only Data | TEXT |
| HEP2 | VersaTerm-PRO - Help | TEXT |
| HLPR | Helix, Double - Customer Helper | APPL |
| HNIX | Helix, Double - Analyzer | APPL |
| hpsl | VideoShop - Visual Info. | vigC |
| HUPD | Helix, Double - Update Collection | APPL |
| IACi | QuicKeys 2 - CEIA | INIT |
| IBEC | Battle Chess - ALLCANM 1 | IPB1 |
| IBEC | Battle Chess - ALLCANM 1 | IPB2 |
| IC2x | In Control 2.0 - Samples | IC2x |
| IFQ1 | IdeaFisher - Edit Q Bank | APPL |
| InTc | InTouch 2.0 - data | ASIl |
| INTU | Quicken - data | BDAT |
| INTU | Quicken - Help | BHLP |
| INTU | Quicken - Supply Order Form | SUPP |
| JAMS | Studio Session - Player | APPL |
| jBox | Sound Edit Pro - Music | jB1 |
| jBox | Sound Edit Pro - Help | jBhp |
| jBox | Sound Edit Pro - Preferences | jBpr |
| JETT | Cricket Paint - Doc | CPNT |
| JOHN | Smart Alarms - Reminders | RMDR |
| JRVL | Vision Lab - Preferences | Pref |
| KAHL | Think C - data | LSD |
| KAHL | Think C - Project | PROJ |
| KAHL | Think C - Debugger | TEST |
| KCFD | Smart Forms - Forms | CFRM |
| keyb | MS Mail - Keyboard | cdev |
| KISS | At Once - data | KISB |
| KISS | At Once - Help | KISD |
| KISS | At Once - Bal. Sheet | KISE |
| KRNE | PageMaker 5.0 - Kern Edit | APPL |
| kver | QuicKeys 2 - Keyset Verifier | APPL |
| L123 | 1-2-3 Files of Various Types | 123F |
| LAND | Frontier - Export | 2CLK |
| LAND | Frontier - Structures | 2CLK |
| LAND | Frontier - Root | TABL |
| LDGb | GreatWorks - Help Balloon | ZHLB |
| LDGd | GreatWorks - Dictionary | ZMDS |
| LDGd | GreatWorks - User Dict. | ZUDT |
| LDGh | GreatWorks - Help | STAK |

| CREATOR CODE | PROGRAM NAME—FILE TYPE | FILE TYPE |
| --- | --- | --- |
| LDGh | GreatWorks - Help System | ZHLS |
| LDGt | GreatWorks - Thesaurus | ZTHS |
| Link | AppleLink - Link Saver | PREF |
| MIST | 1st File - data | 1STD |
| MIST | 1st Base - Text Only Data | TEXT |
| MACA | MacWrite - text-only data | TEXT |
| MACA | MicroPhone II - Help | TEXT |
| MACA | MacWrite - formatted data | WORD |
| MACS | Clipboard File | CLIP |
| MACS | Carbon Copy Mac - ADSP INIT | INIT |
| MAGM | Stuffit Space Saver - MM Extension | FEXT |
| MANA | Daymaker - data | HANK |
| MANA | Daymaker - Forms | MANA |
| MANP | SuperCard - Super Edit | APPL |
| MANP | SuperCard - Preferences | MPPF |
| MCFL | Mac Flow - data | FLCH |
| MCFL | Mac Flow 3.5 - Tutorial | FLCH |
| MCFL | Mac Flow - Stationery | MFST |
| MCV2 | Uninvited - data | MCV2 |
| MCWA | Word 4.0 - Macros | MKDC |
| mdos | Quicken - Connector SCR | TEXT |
| MDPL | MacDraw II - data | DRWG |
| MDPL | FileMaker Pro - Picture | PICT |
| MDPL | MacDraw II - Options | STAT |
| MDRW | MacDraw - data | DRWG |
| MDRW | DesignStudio - Pict | PICT |
| MDRW | Persuasion 2 - Art of Persuasion | PICT |
| MFS4 | MS Flight Simulator 4.0 - Demos | DEMO |
| MFS4 | MS Flight Simulator 4.0 - Aircraft | FLEQ |
| MFS4 | MS Flight Simulator 4.0 - Solutions | MODE |
| MFS4 | MS Flight Simulator 4.0 - Scenery | SCNY |
| MMVW | VideoWorks - data | DATA |
| MMVW | VideoWorks - data | VWSC |
| MNFG | Daymaker - Preferences | PREF |
| MONY | Wealth Builder - Animations | Waim |
| MOVS | MS Mail - Mouse | cdev |
| MPNT | MacPaint - data | PNTG |
| MPRJ | MacProject - data | MPRD |
| MPRX | MacProject II - data | MPRD |
| MRec | Sound Edit Pro - Mac Recorder Driver | INIT |
| MRJN | DesignStudio - Annex | ANNX |
| MRJN | DesignStudio - Dictionary | dct4 |
| MRJN | DesignStudio - Defaults | EEDD |

| CREATOR CODE | PROGRAM NAME—FILE TYPE | FILE TYPE |
|---|---|---|
| MRJN | DesignStudio - Filter | FilT |
| MRJN | DesignStudio - LPD | LPKF |
| MRJN | DesignStudio - Templates | RSGS |
| MRPR | MacProject Pro - data | MPRD |
| MRPR | MacProject Pro - Preferences | MPRE |
| MRPX | MacProject II - Preferences | claP |
| MRSN | Ready, Set, Go! - Dictionary | DCT4 |
| MRSN | Ready, Set, Go! - Hyphenation | HYPH |
| MRSN | Ready, Set, Go! - Data | RSGK |
| MsGW | MS Mail(1) - GW | RDEV |
| MSHE | Microsoft Works 3.0 - Help | HELP |
| MSHE | MS PowerPoint - Help | HELP |
| MSIT | Microsoft Works 3.0 - Thesaurus | WKTC |
| MSIT | Microsoft Works 3.0 - English Thesaurus | WSTF |
| MsMa | MS Mail - MS Mail | RDEV |
| MSPJ | MS Project - Help | HELP |
| MSPJ | MS Project - Calendar | MPC |
| MSPJ | MS Project - Settings | MPF |
| MSPJ | MS Project - data | MPP |
| MSPJ | MS Project - View | MPV |
| MSSP | MS Project - Dictionary | CDIC |
| MSWD | Word 4.0 - Dictionary | DCT5 |
| MSWD | Word 4.0 - Glossary | GLOS |
| MSWD | Apple File Exchange - BCS.WP1 | TEST |
| MSWD | MicroPhone II - Script | TEXT |
| MSWD | Word 4.0 - DATA | WDBN |
| MSWD | MicroPhone II - Auto Scripter | WDBNJ |
| MSWD | Word 4.0 - Help | WHLP |
| MSWD | Word 4.0 - Hyphen | WPRD |
| MSWD | Word 4.0 - Formula Set | WSET |
| MSWK | Microsoft Works 3.0 - Accounts | AWDB |
| MSWK | Microsoft Works 3.0 - Graphics | AWDR |
| MSWK | Microsoft Works 3.0 - Graph | AWSS |
| MSWK | Microsoft Works 3.0 - Write | AWWP |
| MSWK | Microsoft Works 3.0 - Balloon Help | WKHP |
| MSWK | Microsoft Works 3.0 - Conversions | WXFD |
| MTV | JAM Session - Music | JSNG |
| MTVP | JAM Session - Player | APPL |
| MV93 | MacroMedia Director - Movie | MD93 |
| MWII | MacWrite II - Tutorial | MW2D |
| MWII | MacWrite II - Stationery | MW2S |
| MWII | MacWrite II - Hyphen | MW2Z |
| MWII | MacWrite II - Help | STAK |

| CREATOR CODE | PROGRAM NAME—FILE TYPE | FILE TYPE |
|---|---|---|
| MWPR | MacWrite Pro - Balloon Help | BLLN |
| MWPR | MacWrite Pro - US Hypher | HYPH |
| MWPR | MacWrite Pro - data | MWPd |
| MWPR | MacWrite Pro - Help | STAK |
| MXVI | Deja Vu - data | MCVI |
| MYCR | SimEarth | SAVE |
| MYMC | Managing Your Money 4.0 - data | DATA |
| MYOB | MYOB - data | DATA |
| MZPI | Mac Zap - Patches | Zapp |
| nets | AppleTalk Remote - Access | LTMC |
| nEwR | OmniPage Pro - Help | HELP |
| nEwR | OmniPage Pro - US English | MDCT |
| nEwR | OmniPage Pro - User Dictionary | MDUD |
| nEwR | OmniPage Pro - Preferences | PREF |
| NISI | Nisus 3.04 - Hyphenation | HYPT |
| NISI | Nisus 2.0 - Dictionary | MDCT |
| NISI | Nisus 3.04 - Preferences | PRE3 |
| NISI | Nisus 3.04 - Macro | SMAC |
| NISI | Nisus 3.04 - Envelope Stationery | STAT |
| NISI | Nisus 3.04 - Tutorial | TEXT |
| NISI | Nisus 2.0 - Thesaurus | THES |
| NISI | Nisus 2.0 - User Dictionary | UDCT |
| NOSY | Mac Nosy - ROM file | ROM |
| NowT | Now Utilities - Toolbox Preferences | pref |
| NowT | Now Utilities - Toolbox | scri |
| ntk2 | AppleTalk Remote - Remote Only | cdev |
| NUTS | FileMaker - data | NUTD |
| nX^n | WriteNow - Doc | nX^d |
| nX^n | WriteNow - Dictionary | nX^w |
| OM$$ | Omnis3 - data | OM$D |
| OM$$ | Omnis3 - Library | OM$L |
| OM$U | Omnis3 - Utilities | APPL |
| OMEG | Mathematica - data | TEXT |
| ONLC | OnLocation - Preferences | ONLS |
| ONLC | OnLocation - Updater | ONLU |
| ONLC | OnLocation - HD Index | ONLX |
| ONLC | OnLocation - File Kinds | TEXT |
| OnTm | InTouch 2.0 - Reminder | cdev |
| OZIE | Quarterstaff - Stuff | OZYI |
| OZIE | Quarterstaff - Stuff | OZY2 |
| PANT | FullPaint - data | PNTG |
| PARI | InTouch - data | PARM |
| PBA+ | Now Utilities - Scrap Book Preferences | NSDT |

| CREATOR CODE | PROGRAM NAME—FILE TYPE | FILE TYPE |
| --- | --- | --- |
| PCSH | Soft AT - Share PC | APPL |
| PCXT | Soft AT - data | PCDT |
| PJMM | Think Pascal - Interface Library | OBT |
| PLP1 | Persuasion 2 - Dictionary | PRD1 |
| PLP1 | Persuasion - Help | PRH1 |
| PLP1 | Persuasion - Doc | PRS1 |
| PLP1 | Persuasion - Template | PRT1 |
| PLP2 | Persuasion 2 - Samples | GIFf |
| PLP2 | Persuasion 2 - Help | PRH2 |
| PLP2 | Persuasion 2 - AT Kit | PRT2 |
| PLP2 | Persuasion 2 - data | PRT2 |
| PNbe | Norton Utilities 2.0 - Scheduler | INIT |
| PNd1 | Norton Utilities 2.0 - Dial Light | cdev |
| PNda | Norton Utilities 2.0 - Directory Assi. | INIT |
| PNfl | Norton Utilities 2.0 - Floppy Fixer | APPL |
| PNfs | Norton Utilities 2.0 - File Server | cdev |
| PNin | Norton Utilities 2.0 - Installer | APPL |
| PNlp | Norton Utilities 2.0 - Layout | APPL |
| PNnb | Norton Utilities 2.0 - Backup | APPL |
| PNne | Norton Utilities 2.0 - Encryptor | APPL |
| PNnu | Norton Utilities 2.0 - Help | HELP |
| PNnu | Norton Utilities 2.0 - Preferences | pref |
| PNsd | Norton Utilities 2.0 - Speed | APPL |
| PNwi | Norton Utilities 2.0 - Wipe Info. | APPL |
| PPT3 | MS PowerPoint - data | SLD3 |
| PPTV | MS PowerPoint - View | APPL |
| PRGF | Cricket Pictograph - Libraries | PGLB |
| PRGF | Cricket Pictograph - data | STWK |
| PrMr | Fetch | MooV |
| PSHP | Print Shop - Borders | PSBD |
| PSHP | Print Shop - Graphics | PSGR |
| PSHP | Print Shop - Preferences | PSPF |
| PSPT | Apple File Exchange - Settings | STUP |
| PSPT | Lap Link Plus PC - Clipboard | VISA |
| PSPT | Lap Link Plus PC - Translators | VISA |
| PSPT | Word 4.0 - Conv Word Perf | VISA |
| PSPT | Word 4.0 - DCA to RFT/RTF | visa |
| puAB | Address Book Plus - Files | puAB |
| puAB | Address Book Plus - Pref. | puDP |
| PXPM | Typestry - data | PICT |
| Q2$$ | Omnis5 Express - Documentation | Q2$A |
| Q2$$ | Omnis5 Express - data | Q2$D |
| QKba | QuicKeys 2 - Button Action | QKex |

| CREATOR CODE | PROGRAM NAME—FILE TYPE | FILE TYPE |
|---|---|---|
| QKDi | QuicKeys 2 - Display | QKex |
| QKex | QuicKeys - Extension | QKx1 |
| QKK1 | QuicKeys 2 - Keyboard Inte | INIT |
| QKMD | QuicKeys 2 - Menu Decision | QKex |
| QKMP | QuicKeys 2 - QT Mouse | QKex |
| QKMW | QuicKeys 2 - Cursor Wait | QKex |
| QKMW | QuicKeys 2 - Menu Wait | QKex |
| QKpg | QuicKeys 2 - Process Swap | QKex |
| QKQ1 | QuicKeys 2 - Icons | APPL |
| QKRP | QuicKeys 2 - Repeat | QKex |
| QKSC | QuicKeys 2 - Speaker Change | QKex |
| QKWW | QuicKeys 2 - Window Decision | QKex |
| QKx2 | QuicKeys 2 - Panels | QKex |
| QKx3 | QuicKeys 2 - Mousey | QKex |
| QKx4 | QuicKeys 2 - Sound | QKex |
| QKx5 | QuicKeys 2 - Past Ease | QKex |
| QKx6 | QuicKeys 2 - Grab Ease | QKex |
| QKx7 | QuicKeys 2 - Message | QKex |
| QKx8 | QuicKeys 2 - Chopsy | QKex |
| QKx9 | QuicKeys 2 - Location | QKex |
| QKxA | QuicKeys 2 - Type Ease | QKex |
| QKxi | QuicKeys 2 - Extension Manager | APPL |
| QKxW | QuicKeys 2 - Wait | QKex |
| Qky2 | QuicKeys 2 - Help | HELP |
| Qky2 | QuicKeys 2 - Sample Keysets | KEYS |
| QSTL | Quark Style - Dictionary | XDCT |
| QSTL | Quark Style - Help | XHLP |
| QSTL | Quark Style - data | XTMP |
| QxA3 | QuicKeys 2 - Apple Event | QKex |
| QxF2 | QuicKeys 2 - Finder Event | QKex |
| QxS7 | QuicKeys 2 - System 7 Special | QKex |
| QxSk | QuicKeys 2 - Soft Keys | QKex |
| QxUL | QuicKeys 2 - Frontier | QKex |
| ramm | AppleTalk Remote - Aliases | INIT |
| Rem* | Now Up-to-Date - Reminder | cdev |
| RGMA | Geo Query - Help | MAHP |
| RGMA | Geo Query - Special Maps | MASM |
| RGMA | Geo Query - Atlas | MATB |
| Rich | BBEdit - data | TEXT |
| RNST | Managing Your Money - data | DATA |
| RNST | Managing Your Money - Help | MYM1 |
| RNST | Managing Your Money - File | MYM2 |
| RRYD | Red Ryder - RED's Stuff | PDAT |

| CREATOR CODE | PROGRAM NAME—FILE TYPE | FILE TYPE |
|---|---|---|
| RRYD | Red Ryder Services Macro | RRMC |
| RRYD | Red Ryder - data | RRRS |
| RSED | AppleTalk Remote - Resources | rsrc |
| RSLV | MacProject II - Calculator | MRPC |
| RSLV | MacProject II - data | MRPC |
| RSLV | MacProject II - FM Pro Impact | MRPE |
| RSLV | MacProject II - MP Demo | MRPS |
| RSLV | MacProject II - Script | RsCs |
| Rslv | Resolve - Scripts | RsCS |
| Rslv | Resolve - data | Rsws |
| Rslv | Resolve - Help | STAH |
| Rslv | Resolve - Script Source | TEXT |
| RUNT | SuperCard - Global Editors | MDOC |
| rusu | AppleTalk Remote - Setup | cdev |
| RxUP | Retrospect - Updater | APPL |
| Rxvr | Retrospect - Help | Rxv4 |
| Rxvs | Retrospect - Retro.SCSI | APPL |
| S112 | Suitcase 2.0 | Init |
| SANT | SimAnt | SAGM |
| SCAN | Thunderscan - data | SCAN |
| scbk | QuickTime - Scrapbook | dfil |
| ScEa | QuicKeys 2 - Screen Ease | QKex |
| SCOM | Smartcom - data | SCO1 |
| SCOM | Smartcom - Help | SCOO |
| SDQK | QuicKeys 2 - Unstuff | QKex |
| SDQK | StuffIt Deluxe 2.0 - Unstuff | SKex |
| sdQK | QuicKeys 2 - Staff | QKex |
| SFMV | TypeStyler - Smooth Mover | APPL |
| SGas | Swamp Gas - Configuration | CFig |
| SGas | Swamp Gas - Color | CSGp |
| SGas | Swamp Gas - Color Map | CSwp |
| SGas | Swamp Gas - Map USA | Swmp |
| SIDN | StuffIt Deluxe - Installer | APPL |
| SIJ | Mac Nosy - Symbol Tables | appl |
| SIT! | StuffIt Deluxe - Stuffed Files | SITD |
| SIT! | StuffIt Deluxe - Scripts | TEXT |
| SITE | StuffIt Deluxe 2.0 - sit Converter | APPL |
| SITE | StuffIt Space Saver - Stuffit Eng. | APPL |
| Slik | AppleTalk Remote - NMP Link | idev |
| Slik | AppleTalk Remote - Modem | mlts |
| SLiP | VersaTerm-PRO - Control Slip | cdev |
| SLip | VersaTerm-PRO | APPL |
| SMLS | SimLife - Zoo | SLAS |

| CREATOR CODE | PROGRAM NAME—FILE TYPE | FILE TYPE |
|---|---|---|
| SMLS | SimLife - data | SLZO |
| SMLS | SimLife - Animals | SPAL |
| SMLS | SimLife - Plants | SPPL |
| SNap | InTouch 2.0 - Snap* | cdev |
| SOLG | C.A.T. III - Print List | APPL |
| SOLG | C.A.T. III - Template | SIMA |
| SPEK | IntelliDraw - Objects | dSpl |
| SPEK | IntelliDraw - Preferences | SPPF |
| SPEK | IntelliDraw - Defaults | sSpl |
| SPNT | SuperPaint - Preferences | SPPF |
| SPNT | SuperPaint - Doc | SPTG |
| SPTC | OmniPage - Preferences | PRTC |
| SPTC | OmniPage - Translators | TRAN |
| SQPS | Authorware - Tutorial | SQDF |
| SQPS | Authorware - Spell | SQDT |
| SQPS | Authorware - Rules | SQRF |
| SQPS | Authorware - SCM | SQSC |
| SQPS | Authorware - Styles | SQSF |
| SQPS | Authorware - DCds | TEXT |
| SSIW | WordPerfect - Dictionary, user | WPDC |
| SSIW | WordPerfect - Documents | WPDO |
| SSIW | WordPerfect - Dictionary | WPSP |
| SSIW | WordPerfect - Thesaurus | WPTH |
| SSWS | Novell AppWare - Project | SSWP |
| STAX | Sound Edit Pro - Hyper Sound | WILD |
| SWIT | Switcher - data | SWIT |
| SWVL | Swivel 3D - data | SMDL |
| SYBL | Mac Flow - Librarian | APPL |
| SYBL | Mac Flow - Custom Symols | MFSM |
| SYBL | Mac Flow 3.7 - MD Custom Symbols | MFSM |
| SYSC | MS Mail - General | cdev |
| Tac2 | QuicKeys 2 - TAA 2.1.1 | APPL |
| TANK | Think Tank - data | TEXT |
| TBAS | TouchBase - Preferences | PRES |
| TBLX | PageMaker 4.2 - Table Editor | APPL |
| TBUT | TouchBase - Tools | APPL |
| tCAT | C.A.T. III - tCAT | CAT3 |
| tCAT | C.A.T. - data | CATD |
| tCAT | C.A.T. III - Help | CATH |
| tCAT | C.A.T. - Notes | CATN |
| TFFs | VersaTerm-PRO - FP Server | cdev |
| TMKR | Alarming Events - data | RDVS |
| TMKR | Alarming Events - Activities | TEXT |

| CREATOR CODE | PROGRAM NAME—FILE TYPE | FILE TYPE |
|---|---|---|
| TNP2 | Tempo II Macros | TMP |
| TPGE | OmniPage Pro - Graphics Editor | APPL |
| TPLM | Apple File Exchange - Mac/Mac Binary | TEST |
| TRex | PublishIt! Easy - Thesaurus Rex | TRex |
| TRU1 | True Basic - Binder | APPL |
| TRUE | True Basic - Program | TEXT |
| TRUS | TypeReader - Dictionary | TDct |
| TRUS | TypeReader - data | TRDa |
| TRUS | TypeReader - Help | TRHp |
| TRUS | TypeReader - User Dictionary | UDct |
| tsi^ | Laplink Mac III - Init | INIT |
| tsi^ | Laplink Mac III - Start | TEXT |
| TSLR | TypeStyler - AGFA Fonts | TFNT |
| TSLR | TypeStyler - Help | THLP |
| TSLR | TypeStyler - Samples | TSDC |
| TSLR | TypeStyler - Universal | TSDC |
| ttxt | Morph - Picture | Pict |
| ttxt | TeachText | ttro |
| TVOD | QuickTime - Single Player | APPL |
| TVOD | QuickTime - data | MooV |
| TVOD | Video Shop - Hotel | MooV |
| UHRU | Deluxe Music - Music | USC2 |
| UHRU | Deluxe Music - Instruments | UVOX |
| uins | Talking Moose - Talking Finder | uins |
| ULTR | Ultra Paint - Help | BIFF |
| ULTR | Ultra Paint - Color Tables | drwC |
| ULTR | Ultra Paint - Tools | TOOL |
| ULTR | Ultra Paint - data | UPNT |
| ULTR | Ultra Paint - Preferences | UPRF |
| USTD | StuffIt Deluxe 2.0 - Unstuff Deluxe | APPL |
| VETT | Vette - data | DATA |
| VMST | Version Master Data Base | VMDB |
| VMST | Version Master - data | VMPF |
| VMST | Version Master - Preferences | VMPR |
| VRRO | VersaTerm-PRO - Command Set | CMDS |
| VShp | VideoShop - Changes | Vflt |
| VShp | VideoShop - Effects | Vflt |
| VShp | VideoShop - Effects | Vxsn |
| VShp | VideoShop - Effects | Vxsx |
| Vw1K | Virtus' WalkThrough - Library | VLIB |
| Vw1K | Virtus' WalkThrough - data | VMDL |
| WaPr | QuicKeys 2 - Which Printer | QKex |
| WBks | WordPerfect Works - Import Filters | Fltr |

| CREATOR CODE | PROGRAM NAME—FILE TYPE | FILE TYPE |
|---|---|---|
| WBks | WordPerfect Works - USA Spelling | MDCT |
| WBks | WordPerfect Works - Dictionary | UDCT |
| WBks | WordPerfect Works - Thesaurus | WFDT |
| WDGE | Word 5.0 - Spelling | WDIC |
| WDSE | Word 5.0 - Grammar | WDIC |
| WF01 | MacWrite II - US Thesaurus | TH02 |
| WF01 | MacWrite Pro - US Thesaurus | TH02 |
| WFND | MacWrite II - Thesaurus | WFDT |
| WFO1 | Word 4.0 - Thesaurus | THO2 |
| WILD | HyperCard Stack | STAK |
| WK11 | White Knight - Phone Book | PBOK |
| WK11 | White Knight - Proc. Edit | PREP |
| WK11 | White Knight - Stuff | RES2 |
| WK11 | White Knight - Filters | RFLT |
| WK11 | White Knight - Procedure | RRCP |
| wmao | AppleTalk Remote - Responder | INIT |
| WNGZ | Wingz - Help | WZHP |
| WNGZ | Wingz - Script | WZSC |
| WNGZ | Wingz - data | WZSS |
| WORD | Word - File | PCOD |
| WrPa | Retrospect 2.0 - Log | TEXT |
| WrPa | Retrospect 2.0 - Update from 1.3 | WarD |
| WrPa | Retrospect 2.0 - Icon/Conf. | Wrp1 |
| WrPa | Retrospect 2.0 - Help | Wrp4 |
| Wsfl | Quick Letter - Sampler | OLde |
| Wsfl | Quick Letter - Questions & Comments | OLse |
| Wsfl | Quick Letter - Address Book | TEXT |
| WVTX | MacIn Tax - Forms | WVTF |
| WVTX | MacIn Tax - Instructions | WVTI |
| WYSI | Now Utilities - WY S preferences | WDAT |
| XCEL | MS Excel - Chart | MCBN |
| XCEL | MS Excel - Text Only Data | TEXT |
| XCEL | MS Excel - Help | XHLP |
| XCEL | MacSchedule - Export Excel | XLBN |
| XCEL | MS Excel - Worksheet | XLBN |
| XCEL | MS Excel - Resume Excel | XLIN |
| XCEL | MS Excel Setup - Settings | XLPF |
| XCEL | MS Excel - Macro | XLPG |
| XCEL | MS Excel - Plot | XLPG |
| XFRM | QuarkXPress - Frame Editor | APPL |
| XNST | QuarkXPress - Installer | APPL |
| XPR3 | QuarkXPress 3.2 - Frame Editor | APPL |
| XPR3 | QuarkXPress 3.0 - Stuff | CUST |

| CREATOR CODE | PROGRAM NAME—FILE TYPE | FILE TYPE |
|---|---|---|
| XPR3 | QuarkXPress 3.0 - Dictionary | XDCT |
| XPR3 | QuarkXPress 3.0 - Help | XDTA |
| XPR3 | QuarkXPress 3.2 - Frame Editor Helo | XHLP |
| XPR3 | QuarkXPress 3.0 - Output Req. Temdp. | XTMP |
| XPR3 | QuarkXPress 3.0 - Balloon Help | XTRb |
| XPRS | QuarkXPress - Filters | CUST |
| XPRS | QuarkXPress - Dictionary | XDCT |
| XPRS | QuarkXPress - data | XDTA |
| XPRS | QuarkXPress - Help | XHLP |
| XPRT | Studio Session - Songs | XSNG |
| ZEBR | GreatWorks - Letter | ZWRT |
| ZWBR | GreatWorks - Statement | ZCAL |

## TABLE A–2. COMMON MACINTOSH FILE TYPES AND CREATOR CODES IN ALPHABETICAL ORDER BY PROGRAM NAME

| PROGRAM NAME | CREATOR CODE | FILE TYPE |
|---|---|---|
| 1-2-3 Files of Various Types | L123 | 123F |
| 1st Aid - Extracted Text | 1Aid | TEXT |
| 1st Aid - Recovered File | 1Aid | GOOD |
| 1st Aid - Recovered Fragment | 1Aid | FRAG |
| 1st Base - Text Only Data | MIST | TEXT |
| 1st Desk - Settings | BBSR | BBSR |
| 1st File - data | MIST | 1STD |
| 4th Dimension - data | 4D02 | data |
| 4th Dimension - Flag | 4D02 | FLAG |
| 4th Dimension - Index | 4D02 | INDX |
| 4th Dimension - Project | 4D02 | BAS2 |
| 4th Dimension 2.0 - data | 4DO3 | 4DES |
| 4th Dimension 2.0 - Templates | 4DO3 | 4DET |
| Access PC - data | AcPC | APCd |
| Acta file | ACTA | OTLN |
| Address Book Plus - Files | puAB | puAB |
| Address Book Plus - Pref. | puAB | puDP |
| Address List | adbk | adli |
| Adobe Type Manager | Famx | APPL |
| Adobe Type Manager - ATM 68000 | ATMC | ATMD |
| Adobe Type Manager - Type Reunion | ATR | INIT |
| Adobe Type Mgr. - Fonts | ASPF | LWFN |

| PROGRAM NAME | CREATOR CODE | FILE TYPE |
|---|---|---|
| After Dark - files | ADrk | ADgm |
| Alarming Events - Activities | TMKR | TEXT |
| Alarming Events - data | TMKR | RDVS |
| Apple File Exchange - BCS.RTF | ???? | TEST |
| Apple File Exchange - BCS.WP1 | MSWD | TEST |
| Apple File Exchange - DT Translation | DVDT | MLSD |
| Apple File Exchange - Mac/Mac Binary | TPLM | TEST |
| Apple File Exchange - Settings | PSPT | STUP |
| AppleLink - CCL | GEOL | PETE |
| AppleLink - Help | GEOL | HLPF |
| AppleLink - Link Saver | Link | PREF |
| AppleLink - Resources | GEOL | rsrc |
| AppleTalk Remote - Access | nets | LTMC |
| AppleTalk Remote - Aliases | ramm | INIT |
| AppleTalk Remote - EtherNet 2 | et20 | cdev |
| AppleTalk Remote - Modem | Slik | mlts |
| AppleTalk Remote - Network | atdv | cdev |
| AppleTalk Remote - NMP Link | Slik | idev |
| AppleTalk Remote - Remote Only | ntk2 | cdev |
| AppleTalk Remote - Resources | RSED | rsrc |
| AppleTalk Remote - Responder | wmao | INIT |
| AppleTalk Remote - Script | bjbc | bjbc |
| AppleTalk Remote - Setup | rusu | cdev |
| AppWare - Project | SSWS | SSWP |
| Astound - English Dict. | GDPS | GDIC |
| Astound - Player | ASPL | APPL |
| Astound - to AGX-Mac | AGXS | APPL |
| At Once - Bal. Sheet | KISS | KISE |
| At Once - data | KISS | KISB |
| At Once - Help | KISS | KISD |
| Authorware - DCds | SQPS | TEXT |
| Authorware - Rules | SQPS | SQRF |
| Authorware - SCM | SQPS | SQSC |
| Authorware - Spell | SQPS | SQDT |
| Authorware - Styles | SQPS | SQSF |
| Authorware - Tutorial | SQPS | SQDF |
| Auto Doubler - data | DDAP | ADDA |
| Auto Doubler - Desk Top Reset | DTRS | APPL |
| Auto Doubler - Expand | DDAP | APPL |
| Auto Doubler - Re BNDLer | ???? | APPL |
| Auto Doubler - Verify/Rep | DDRP | APPL |
| Battle Chess - ALLCANM 1 | IBEC | IPB1 |
| Battle Chess - ALLCANM 1 | IBEC | IPB2 |

| Program Name | Creator Code | File Type |
|---|---|---|
| BBEdit - data | Rich | TEXT |
| Binhex - data | BnHq | TEXT |
| C.A.T. - data | tCAT | CATD |
| C.A.T. - Notes | tCAT | CATN |
| C.A.T. III - Help | tCAT | CATH |
| C.A.T. III - Print List | SOLG | APPL |
| C.A.T. III - tCAT | tCAT | CAT3 |
| C.A.T. III - Template | SOLG | SIMA |
| Calendar Maker - Icon Mover | CECM | APPL |
| Calendar Maker - Icons | CEIM | CEIF |
| Calendar Maker - Paint | CEBN | PNTG |
| Can Opener - Library | ec12 | oLIB |
| Can Opener - State | ec12 | caoS |
| Canvas - Color Tables | DAD2 | drwC |
| Canvas - data | DAD2 | drw2 |
| Canvas - Dictionary | DAD2 | CONF |
| Canvas - Help | DAD2 | BIFF |
| Canvas - Macro | DAD2 | Ma3R |
| Canvas - Preferences | DAD2 | def2 |
| Carbon Copy Mac - ADSP INIT | MACS | INIT |
| Carbon Copy Mac - Help | CCMa | CCHP |
| Carbon Copy Mac - Serial Setup | CCMa | PORT |
| CE Toolbox | CEtb | INIT |
| ClarisWorks 2 - Color Gradient | BOBO | dCol |
| ClarisWorks 2 - data Data Base | BOBO | CWDB |
| ClarisWorks 2 - data Spreadsheet | BOBO | CWSS |
| ClarisWorks 2 - data Word | BOBO | CWGR |
| ClarisWorks 2 - Dictionary (Main) | CSpt | QMdt |
| ClarisWorks 2 - Dictionary (User) | CSpt | CUdt |
| ClarisWorks 2 - Extend | Clrs | CLRS |
| ClarisWorks 2 - Name & Address | BOBO | sWDB |
| ClarisWorks 2 - Stationery | BOBO | sWWP |
| ClickPaste - Object | CrCr | CpCf |
| Clipboard File | MACS | CLIP |
| Color MacCheese - data | CMCÆ | PICT |
| Color MacCheese - Preferences | CMCÆ | CMCπ |
| Common Ground | CGMK | PREF |
| Common Ground - Auto Maker | CGMK | APPL |
| Common Ground - CG Maker | CGMK | APPL |
| Compact Pro - Archive | CPC* | PACT |
| Cricket Color Paint - data | DECO | CRCP |
| Cricket Data III - data | dTbk | dbTX |
| Cricket Graph - data | CGRF | CGTX |

| PROGRAM NAME | CREATOR CODE | FILE TYPE |
|---|---|---|
| Cricket Graph III - data | CRGR | CRGF |
| Cricket Graph III - data data | CRGR | CGDW |
| Cricket Graph III - data Graph | CRGR | CGGW |
| Cricket Graph III - Help | CRGR | HELP |
| Cricket Graph III - Palettes | CRGR | CPAL |
| Cricket Graph III - Preferences | CRGR | CGPR |
| Cricket Paint - Doc | JETT | CPNT |
| Cricket Pictograph - data | PRGF | STWK |
| Cricket Pictograph - Libraries | PRGF | PGLB |
| Cricket Presents - data | CRPR | CRTM |
| DA Mover - data | DAMV | DESK |
| DAC Easy Light - data | DACL | CHRT |
| DAC Easy Light - Help | DACL | DHlp |
| Darwin's Dilemma - Sample | AOp2 | DDGM |
| Darwin's Dilemma - Standard | AOp2 | DDST |
| DateBook - Icon Library | dbIN | INIT |
| DateBook - Preferences | DtBk | PREF |
| Daymaker - Alarm | DMOV | DFIL |
| Daymaker - data | MANA | HANK |
| Daymaker - Forms | MANA | MANA |
| Daymaker - Preferences | MNFG | PREF |
| dBase Mac | ASBM | ADBE |
| Deja Vu - data | MXV1 | MCV1 |
| DeltaGraph - 3D Perspective | DGRH | DGRD |
| DeltaGraph - Color | DGRH | SPID |
| DeltaGraph - Delta Sim | aCf2 | LWFN |
| DeltaGraph - Help | DGRH | HELP |
| DeltaGraph - Library | DGRH | LIBR |
| DeltaGraph - Preferences | DGRH | PREF |
| DeltaGraph Pro - Dictionary | DGRH | DGmD |
| DeltaGraph Pro - Library | DGRH | LBR2 |
| DeltaGraph Pro - Stationery | DGRH | DGPD |
| DeltaGraph Pro - Tutorial | DGRH | DSPF |
| DeltaGraph Pro - User Dictionary | DGRH | DGuD |
| Deluxe Music - Instruments | UHRU | UVOX |
| Deluxe Music - Music | UHRU | USC2 |
| DesignStudio - Annex | MRJN | ANNX |
| DesignStudio - Defaults | MRJN | EEDD |
| DesignStudio - Dictionary | MRJN | dct4 |
| DesignStudio - Filter | MRJN | FilT |
| DesignStudio - LPD | MRJN | LPKF |
| DesignStudio - Pict | MDRW | PICT |
| DesignStudio - Riff | FSPE | RIFF |

| PROGRAM NAME | CREATOR CODE | FILE TYPE |
|---|---|---|
| DesignStudio - Templates | MRJN | RSGS |
| DeskPaint - Color | Dpnt | Dpol |
| DeskPaint - data | Dpnt | PNTG |
| DeskPaint - Help | Dpnt | ZHLP |
| Digital Darkroom | ALZI | ALZC |
| Digital Darkroom - data | ALZI | ACMP |
| Digital Darkroom - Drawings | DIDR | DIDA |
| Digital Darkroom - Installer | ALZI | APPL |
| Director - Movie | MV93 | MD93 |
| DiskTop - CE TB Preferences | CEtb | DATA |
| DiskTop - CE Toolbox | CEtb | INIT |
| DiskTop - Extras | DkTP | INIT |
| DiskTop - Init | CELD | INIT |
| DiskTop - Preferences | dkpt | Pfef |
| Dollars & Sense - data | DAS | DASD |
| Dollars & Sense 4.1 - data | EGAP | EGAD |
| Dollars & Sense 4.1 - Help | EGAP | EGAH |
| Dynodex - Apple Image | DYNO | DYED |
| Dynodex - Control Panel | DnPg | cdev |
| Dynodex - DA | DMOV | DFIL |
| Dynodex - data | DYNO | DYDB |
| Dynodex - Day Timer | DYNO | DYAD |
| Dynodex - Help | DYNO | DYHP |
| Dynodex - Paper | DnPg | VLnf |
| Dynodex - Paper Direct | DYNO | DYLB |
| Dynodex - Portfolio | DYNO | JNPD |
| Dynodex - Time Design | DYNO | DYAD |
| Dynodex 3.0 - Address Change | DYNO | DYMM |
| Dynodex 3.0 - Co Star Layout | DYNO | DYEN |
| Easy Envelopes | EEfi | rsrc |
| Fetch | PrMr | MooV |
| FileMaker - data | NUTS | NUTD |
| FileMaker Plus - data | FMKR | FMKD |
| FileMaker Pro - Claris Help | ClrH | HCOD |
| FileMaker Pro - Dictionary | CSpf | CMdt |
| FileMaker Pro - Help | FMPR | STAX |
| FileMaker Pro - Picture | MDPL | PICT |
| FileMaker Pro - Template | FMPR | FMPR |
| FileMaker Pro 2.0 - Data | FMPR | FMPR |
| FileMaker Pro 2.0 - Events | FMPR | FMPR |
| FileMaker Pro 2.0 - User Dictionary | CSpf | CUdt |
| FirstClass - Bin Hex | BnHg | APPL |
| FirstClass - Local | FCui | FCsf |

| PROGRAM NAME | CREATOR CODE | FILE TYPE |
|---|---|---|
| FirstClass - Phone Book | FCui | FCsf |
| FirstClass - Settings | aust | APPL |
| FoxPro 2.5 - Database File | FOXX | F+DB |
| FoxPro 2.5 - Index File | FOXX | FCDX |
| FoxPro 2.5 - Program File | FOXX | F+PR |
| FoxPro 2.5 - Form File | FOXX | F+DT |
| FrameMaker - Dictionary | Fram | FUdc |
| FrameMaker - Help | Fram | FHlp |
| Freedom of the Press - Configure | EDIT | TEXT |
| Freedom of the Press - Installer | ???? | APPL |
| Freedom of the Press - Language | FRCS | FPER |
| Freedom of the Press - Outline | FRCS | FPDR |
| Freedom of the Press - Spooler 1.1 | FRDP | APPL |
| Freedom of the Press - Spooler 1.2 | FRPS | APPL |
| Freedom of the Press 4.0 - Metrics | FRCS | FPDF |
| FreeHand - data | aca3 | acf3 |
| Frontier - Bar Chart | BARC | APPL |
| Frontier - Data Base | DOCS | DBAS |
| Frontier - Export | LAND | 2CLK |
| Frontier - Finder Application | fMNU | APPL |
| Frontier - Finder Menu | fmcc | INIT |
| Frontier - Preferences | fmcc | FMPR |
| Frontier - Root | LAND | TABL |
| Frontier - Structures | LAND | 2CLK |
| Full Impact - data | GLAS | ADGH |
| Full Impact - Macros | GLAS | GMAC |
| Full Write Prof. - data | FWRT | FWRT |
| Full Write Prof. - Dictionary | FWRT | FWDI |
| Full Write Prof. - Glossary | FWRT | FWGL |
| Full Write Prof. - Stationery | FWRT | FWST |
| Full Write Prof. - Thesaurus | FWRT | FWTI |
| Full Write Prof. - User Dictionary | FWRT | FWUD |
| FullPaint - data | PANT | PNTG |
| Geo Query - Atlas | RGMA | MATB |
| Geo Query - Help | RGMA | MAHP |
| Geo Query - Special Maps | RGMA | MASM |
| GreatWorks - Dictionary | LDGd | ZMDS |
| GreatWorks - Help | LDGh | STAK |
| GreatWorks - Help Balloon | LDGb | ZHLB |
| GreatWorks - Help System | LDGh | ZHLS |
| GreatWorks - Letter | ZEBR | ZWRT |
| GreatWorks - Statement | ZWBR | ZCAL |
| GreatWorks - Thesaurus | LDGt | ZTHS |

| Program Name | Creator Code | File Type |
|---|---|---|
| GreatWorks - User Dict. | LDGd | ZUDT |
| Helix - Formatted Data | HELX | HEAP |
| Helix - Help | HELX | HEXT |
| Helix - Text Only Data | HELX | TEXT |
| Helix, Double - Analyzer | HNIX | APPL |
| Helix, Double - Customer Helper | HLPR | APPL |
| Helix, Double - data | HELX | HEAP |
| Helix, Double - Update Collection | HUPD | APPL |
| HyperCard Stack | WILD | STAK |
| IdeaFisher - Edit Q Bank | IFQ1 | APPL |
| In Control - data | flip | FLIP |
| In Control - Extend | Clro | CLRS |
| In Control - Samples | flip | FLIP |
| In Control - Translators | Clro | Fltr |
| In Control 2.0 - Samples | IC2x | IC2x |
| InitPicker - Sound | Aard | IPsn |
| IntelliDraw - Defaults | SPEK | sSp1 |
| IntelliDraw - Objects | SPEK | dSp1 |
| IntelliDraw - Preferences | SPEK | SPPF |
| InTouch - DA | DMOV | DFIL |
| InTouch - data | PAR1 | PARM |
| InTouch - Network - DA | DMOV | DFIL |
| InTouch 2.0 - data | InTc | ASII |
| InTouch 2.0 - Reminder | OnTm | cdev |
| InTouch 2.0 - Snap* | SNap | cdev |
| JAM Session - Music | MTV | JSNG |
| JAM Session - Player | MTVP | APPL |
| Lap Link Plus PC - Cable to Pc | DVPC | MLSD |
| Lap Link Plus PC - Clipboard | PSPT | VISA |
| Lap Link Plus PC - Translators | PSPT | VISA |
| Laplink Mac III - Init | tsi^ | INIT |
| Laplink Mac III - Start | tsi^ | TEXT |
| MacDraw - data | MDRW | DRWG |
| MacDraw II - data | MDPL | DRWG |
| MacDraw II - Options | MDPL | STAT |
| MacDraw Pro - data | dPro | dDoc |
| MacDraw Pro - Pantone Palettes | dPro | dCol |
| MacDraw Pro - Slides | dPro | dLib |
| MacDraw Pro - Stationery | dPro | dSta |
| Mac Envelope - Lists | ENV5 | EV4Z |
| Mac Envelope - Templates | ENV5 | ENDF |
| Mac Flow - Custom Symols | SYBL | MFSM |
| Mac Flow - data | MCFL | FLCH |

| Program Name | Creator Code | File Type |
|---|---|---|
| Mac Flow - Librarian | SYBL | APPL |
| Mac Flow - Stationery | MCFL | MFST |
| Mac Flow 3.5 - Tutorial | MCFL | FLCH |
| Mac Flow 3.7 - MD Custom Symbols | SYBL | MFSM |
| MacIn Tax - Forms | WVTX | WVTF |
| MacIn Tax - Instructions | WVTX | WVTI |
| Mac Nosy - ROM file | NOSY | ROM |
| Mac Nosy - Symbol Tables | SIJ | appl |
| MacPaint - data | MPNT | PNTG |
| MacProject - data | MPRJ | MPRD |
| MacProject II - Calculator | RSLV | MRPC |
| MacProject II - data | MPRX | MPRD |
| MacProject II - data | RSLV | MRPC |
| MacProject II - FM Export Data | BAT | TEXT |
| MacProject II - FM Pro Impact | RSLV | MRPE |
| MacProject II - MP Demo | RSLV | MRPS |
| MacProject II - Preferences | MRPX | claP |
| MacProject II - Script | RSLV | RsCs |
| MacProject Pro - data | MRPR | MPRD |
| MacProject Pro - Preferences | MRPR | MPRE |
| MacSchedule - data | GAnt | EASy |
| MacSchedule - Export Excel | XCEL | XLBN |
| MacWrite - formatted data | MACA | WORD |
| MacWrite - text-only data | MACA | TEXT |
| MacWrite II - Claris Help | ClnH | HCOD |
| MacWrite II - Dictionary | CDpf | CMdt |
| MacWrite II - Dictionary, UK | CDpf | CMut |
| MacWrite II - Help | MWII | STAK |
| MacWrite II - Hyphen | MWII | MW2Z |
| MacWrite II - Stationery | MWII | MW2S |
| MacWrite II - Thesaurus | WFND | WFDT |
| MacWrite II - Tutorial | MWII | MW2D |
| MacWrite II - US Thesaurus | WF01 | TH02 |
| MacWrite Pro - Balloon Help | MWPR | BLLN |
| MacWrite Pro - Claris Help System | ClrH | HCOD |
| MacWrite Pro - data | MWPR | MWPd |
| MacWrite Pro - Help | MWPR | STAK |
| MacWrite Pro - Main Dictionary | CSpf | CMdp |
| MacWrite Pro - US Hypher | MWPR | HYPH |
| MacWrite Pro - US Thesaurus | WF01 | TH02 |
| MacWrite Pro - User Dictionary | CSpf | CUdt |
| Mac Zap - Patches | MZP1 | Zapp |
| Managing Your Money - data | RNST | DATA |

| Program Name | Creator Code | File Type |
|---|---|---|
| Managing Your Money - File | RNST | MYM2 |
| Managing Your Money - Help | RNST | MYM1 |
| Managing Your Money 4.0 - data | MYMC | DATA |
| Mathematica - data | OMEG | TEXT |
| MicroPhone - data | DFBO | DFBA |
| MicroPhone II - Auto Scripter | MSWD | WDBNJ |
| MicroPhone II - Help | MACA | TEXT |
| MicroPhone II - Modem | DFBO | DFBB |
| MicroPhone II - Script | MSWD | TEXT |
| Microsoft Works 3.0 - Accounts | MSWK | AWDB |
| Microsoft Works 3.0 - Balloon Help | MSWK | WKHP |
| Microsoft Works 3.0 - Conversions | MSWK | WXFD |
| Microsoft Works 3.0 - English Thesaurus | MSIT | WSTF |
| Microsoft Works 3.0 - Graph | MSWK | AWSS |
| Microsoft Works 3.0 - Graphics | MSWK | AWDR |
| Microsoft Works 3.0 - Help | MSHE | HELP |
| Microsoft Works 3.0 - Thesaurus | MSIT | WKTC |
| Microsoft Works 3.0 - Write | MSWK | AWWP |
| Morph - data | ARQM | MORF |
| Morph - Photo | ARQM | MORF |
| Morph - Picture | ttxt | Pict |
| MS Excel - Chart | XCEL | MCBN |
| MS Excel - Help | XCEL | XHLP |
| MS Excel - Macro | XCEL | XLPG |
| MS Excel - Plot | XCEL | XLPG |
| MS Excel - Resume Excel | XCEL | XLIN |
| MS Excel - Text Only Data | XCEL | TEXT |
| MS Excel - Worksheet | XCEL | XLBN |
| MS Excel Setup - Settings | XCEL | XLPF |
| MS File - Form | FILE | FORM |
| MS File - Formatted Data | FILE | ISAM |
| MS File - Help | FILE | FHLP |
| MS Flight Simulator 4.0 - Aircraft | MFS4 | FLEQ |
| MS Flight Simulator 4.0 - Demos | MFS4 | DEMO |
| MS Flight Simulator 4.0 - Scenery | MFS4 | SCNY |
| MS Flight Simulator 4.0 - Solutions | MFS4 | MODE |
| MS Mail - General | SYSC | cdev |
| MS Mail - Keyboard | keyb | cdev |
| MS Mail - Mouse | MOVS | cdev |
| MS Mail - MS Mail | MsMa | RDEV |
| MS Mail(1) - GW | MsGW | RDEV |
| MS PowerPoint - data | PPT3 | SLD3 |
| MS PowerPoint - Help | MSHE | HELP |

| PROGRAM NAME | CREATOR CODE | FILE TYPE |
| --- | --- | --- |
| MS PowerPoint - View | PPTV | APPL |
| MS Project - Calendar | MSPJ | MPC |
| MS Project - data | MSPJ | MPP |
| MS Project - Dictionary | MSSP | CDIC |
| MS Project - Help | MSPJ | HELP |
| MS Project - Settings | MSPJ | MPF |
| MS Project - View | MSPJ | MPV |
| MYOB - data | MYOB | DATA |
| Nisus 2.0 - Dictionary | NISI | MDCT |
| Nisus 2.0 - Thesaurus | NISI | THES |
| Nisus 2.0 - User Dictionary | NISI | UDCT |
| Nisus 3.04 - Envelope Stationery | NISI | STAT |
| Nisus 3.04 - Hyphenation | NISI | HYPT |
| Nisus 3.04 - Import | ALD4 | FCOD |
| Nisus 3.04 - Macro | NISI | SMAC |
| Nisus 3.04 - Preferences | NISI | PRE3 |
| Nisus 3.04 - Tutorial | NISI | TEXT |
| Norton Utilities 2.0 - Backup | PNnb | APPL |
| Norton Utilities 2.0 - Dial Light | PNdl | cdev |
| Norton Utilities 2.0 - Directory Assi. | PNda | INIT |
| Norton Utilities 2.0 - Encryptor | PNne | APPL |
| Norton Utilities 2.0 - Fast Find | DMOV | DFIL |
| Norton Utilities 2.0 - File Server | PNfs | cdev |
| Norton Utilities 2.0 - Floppy Fixer | PNfl | APPL |
| Norton Utilities 2.0 - Help | PNnu | HELP |
| Norton Utilities 2.0 - Installer | PNin | APPL |
| Norton Utilities 2.0 - Layout | PNlp | APPL |
| Norton Utilities 2.0 - Preferences | PNnu | pref |
| Norton Utilities 2.0 - Scheduler | PNbe | INIT |
| Norton Utilities 2.0 - Speed | PNsd | APPL |
| Norton Utilities 2.0 - Wipe Info. | PNwi | APPL |
| Now Up-to-Date - Appointment Book | Cal* | C*DR |
| Now Up-to-Date - Calendar | Cal* | C*DB |
| Now Up-to-Date - Reminder | Rem* | cdev |
| Now Up-to-Date - Server | C*SS | INIT |
| Now Utilities - SB Extra | dMRN | ECRI |
| Now Utilities - SB Preferences | dMRN | dMDT |
| Now Utilities - Scrap Book Preferences | PBA+ | NSDT |
| Now Utilities - Toolbox | NowT | scri |
| Now Utilities - Toolbox Preferences | NowT | pref |
| Now Utilities - WY S preferences | WYSI | WDAT |
| OmniPage - Preferences | SPTC | PRTC |
| OmniPage - Translators | SPTC | TRAN |

| PROGRAM NAME | CREATOR CODE | FILE TYPE |
|---|---|---|
| OmniPage Pro - Graphics Editor | TPGE | APPL |
| OmniPage Pro - Help | nEwR | HELP |
| OmniPage Pro - Preferences | nEwR | PREF |
| OmniPage Pro - US English | nEwR | MDCT |
| OmniPage Pro - User Dictionary | nEwR | MDUD |
| Omnis3 - data | OM$$ | OM$D |
| Omnis3 - Library | OM$$ | OM$L |
| Omnis3 - Utilities | OM$U | APPL |
| Omnis5 Express - data | Q2$$ | Q2$D |
| Omnis5 Express - Documentation | Q2$$ | Q2$A |
| OnLocation - DA | DMOV | DFIL |
| OnLocation - File Kinds | ONLC | TEXT |
| OnLocation - HD Index | ONLC | ONLX |
| OnLocation - Preferences | ONLC | ONLS |
| OnLocation - Updater | ONLC | ONLU |
| OverVUE - Formatted Data | DVUE | DVSH |
| OverVUE - Text data | DVUE | TEXT |
| PageMaker 4.0 - Ald Eng | ALD4 | ALC4 |
| PageMaker 4.0 - Colors | ALD4 | BClf |
| PageMaker 4.0 - Filters | ALD4 | FCOD |
| PageMaker 4.0 - Kern Tracks | ALD4 | ALQ4 |
| PageMaker 4.0 - Prep | ALD4 | ALDP |
| PageMaker 4.2 - Additions | ALD4 | ALD4 |
| PageMaker 4.2 - Dictionary Editor | ALD4 | AMD4 |
| PageMaker 4.2 - Dictionary | ALD4 | AND4 |
| PageMaker 4.2 - Filters | ALD4 | FCD4 |
| PageMaker 4.2 - Help | ALD4 | PRH1 |
| PageMaker 4.2 - Resources | ALD4 | ALR4 |
| PageMaker 4.2 - Table Editor | TBLX | APPL |
| PageMaker 5.0 - Additions | ALD5 | ALD5 |
| PageMaker 5.0 - Color | ALD5 | BClf |
| PageMaker 5.0 - Filter | ALD5 | FLT3 |
| PageMaker 5.0 - Help | ALD5 | PRH1 |
| PageMaker 5.0 - Kern Edit | KRNE | APPL |
| PageMaker 5.0 - Other Stuff | ALD5 | ALD5 |
| PageMaker 5.0 - PM5 Defaults | ALD5 | ALF5 |
| PageMaker 5.0 - Templates | ???? | TEXT |
| Persuasion - Doc | PLP1 | PRS1 |
| Persuasion - Help | PLP1 | PRH1 |
| Persuasion - Template | PLP1 | PRT1 |
| Persuasion 2 - Art of Persuasion | MDRW | PICT |
| Persuasion 2 - AT Kit | PLP2 | PRT2 |
| Persuasion 2 - data | PLP2 | PRT2 |

| Program Name | Creator Code | File Type |
|---|---|---|
| Persuasion 2 - Dictionary | PLP1 | PRD1 |
| Persuasion 2 - Help | PLP2 | PRH2 |
| Persuasion 2 - Samples | PLP2 | GIFf |
| Print Shop - Borders | PSHP | PSBD |
| Print Shop - Graphics | PSHP | PSGR |
| Print Shop - Preferences | PSHP | PSPF |
| PublishIt Easy! - data | 2CTY | TEXT |
| PublishIt Easy! - Dictionary | 2CTY | SSPL |
| PublishIt Easy! - Document | 2CTY | SPVB |
| PublishIt Easy! - Help | 2CTY | SHLP |
| PublishIt Easy! - Hyphenation | 2CTY | SHYP |
| PublishIt Easy! - Input Filter | 2CTY | ROFT |
| PublishIt Easy! - Layouts | 2CTY | SPUC |
| PublishIt Easy! - Thesaurus Rex | TRex | TRex |
| Quark Style - data | QSTL | XTMP |
| Quark Style - Dictionary | QSTL | XDCT |
| Quark Style - Help | QSTL | XHLP |
| QuarkXPress - data | XPRS | XDTA |
| QuarkXPress - Dictionary | XPRS | XDCT |
| QuarkXPress - Filters | XPRS | CUST |
| QuarkXPress - Frame Editor | XFRM | APPL |
| QuarkXPress - Help | XPRS | XHLP |
| QuarkXPress - Installer | XNST | APPL |
| QuarkXPress 3.0 - Balloon Help | XPR3 | XTRb |
| QuarkXPress 3.0 - Dictionary | XPR3 | XDCT |
| QuarkXPress 3.0 - Help | XPR3 | XDTA |
| QuarkXPress 3.0 - Output Req. Temdp. | XPR3 | XTMP |
| QuarkXPress 3.0 - Stuff | XPR3 | CUST |
| QuarkXPress 3.2 - Frame Editor | XPR3 | APPL |
| QuarkXPress 3.2 - Frame Editor Helo | XPR3 | XHLP |
| Quarterstaff - Stuff | OZIE | OZY1 |
| Quarterstaff - Stuff | OZIE | OZY2 |
| QuicKeys - Extension | QKex | QKx1 |
| QuicKeys 2 - Apple Event | QxA3 | QKex |
| QuicKeys 2 - Button Action | QKba | QKex |
| QuicKeys 2 - CEIA | IACi | INIT |
| QuicKeys 2 - Chopsy | QKx8 | QKex |
| QuicKeys 2 - Configure TB | eeTB | APPL |
| QuicKeys 2 - Cursor Wait | QKMW | QKex |
| QuicKeys 2 - Dialog Keys | CEKM | cdev |
| QuicKeys 2 - Dis. Mounty | DmEa | QKex |
| QuicKeys 2 - Display | QKDi | QKex |
| QuicKeys 2 - Extension Manager | QKxi | APPL |

| PROGRAM NAME | CREATOR CODE | FILE TYPE |
|---|---|---|
| QuicKeys 2 - Finder Event | QxF2 | QKex |
| QuicKeys 2 - Frontier | QxUL | QKex |
| QuicKeys 2 - Grab Ease | QKx6 | QKex |
| QuicKeys 2 - Heap Framer | Heap | APPL |
| QuicKeys 2 - Help | Qky2 | HELP |
| QuicKeys 2 - Icons | QKQl | APPL |
| QuicKeys 2 - Installer | bbkr | APPL |
| QuicKeys 2 - Keyboard Inte | QKKl | INIT |
| QuicKeys 2 - Keyset Verifier | kver | APPL |
| QuicKeys 2 - Location | QKx9 | QKex |
| QuicKeys 2 - Menu Decision | QKMD | QKex |
| QuicKeys 2 - Menu Wait | QKMW | QKex |
| QuicKeys 2 - Message | QKx7 | QKex |
| QuicKeys 2 - Mousey | QKx3 | QKex |
| QuicKeys 2 - Panels | QKx2 | QKex |
| QuicKeys 2 - Past Ease | QKx5 | QKex |
| QuicKeys 2 - Power Book | CxPB | QKex |
| QuicKeys 2 - Process Swap | QKpg | QKex |
| QuicKeys 2 - QT Mouse | QKMP | QKex |
| QuicKeys 2 - Repeat | QKRP | QKex |
| QuicKeys 2 - Sample Keysets | Qky2 | KEYS |
| QuicKeys 2 - Screen Ease | ScEa | QKex |
| QuicKeys 2 - Soft Keys | QxSk | QKex |
| QuicKeys 2 - Sound | QKx4 | QKex |
| QuicKeys 2 - Speaker Change | QKSC | QKex |
| QuicKeys 2 - Staff | sdQK | QKex |
| QuicKeys 2 - System 7 Special | QxS7 | QKex |
| QuicKeys 2 - TAA 2.1.1 | Tac2 | APPL |
| QuicKeys 2 - Template Printer | GDG2 | APPL |
| QuicKeys 2 - Tool Box | CEtb | INIT |
| QuicKeys 2 - Type Ease | QKxA | QKex |
| QuicKeys 2 - Unstuff | SDQK | QKex |
| QuicKeys 2 - Wait | QKxW | QKex |
| QuicKeys 2 - Which Printer | WaPr | QKex |
| QuicKeys 2 - Window Decision | QKWW | QKex |
| Quick Letter - Address Book | Wsfl | TEXT |
| Quick Letter - Questions & Comments | Wsfl | OLse |
| Quick Letter - Sampler | Wsfl | OLde |
| QuickMail - Help | CELM | QMHP |
| QuickMail - Resources | CELM | CCde |
| QuickMail Remote - Help | CEDA | QMHP |
| QuickTime - data | TVOD | MooV |
| QuickTime - Scrapbook | scbk | dfil |

| PROGRAM NAME | CREATOR CODE | FILE TYPE |
|---|---|---|
| QuickTime - Single Player | TVOD | APPL |
| Quicken - Connector SCR | mdos | TEXT |
| Quicken - data | INTU | BDAT |
| Quicken - Help | INTU | BHLP |
| Quicken - Home Categories | ???? | TEXT |
| Quicken - Supply Order Form | INTU | SUPP |
| Ready, Set, Go! - Data | MRSN | RSGK |
| Ready, Set, Go! - Dictionary | MRSN | DCT4 |
| Ready, Set, Go! - Hyphenation | MRSN | HYPH |
| Red Ryder - data | RRYD | RRRS |
| Red Ryder - RED's Stuff | RRYD | PDAT |
| Red Ryder Services Macro | RRYD | RRMC |
| Resolve - data | Rslv | Rsws |
| Resolve - Help | Rslv | STAH |
| Resolve - Script Source | Rslv | TEXT |
| Resolve - Scripts | Rslv | RsCS |
| Retrospect - Help | Rxvr | Rxv4 |
| Retrospect - Retro.SCSI | Rxvs | APPL |
| Retrospect - Updater | RxUP | APPL |
| Retrospect 2.0 - Help | WrPa | Wrp4 |
| Retrospect 2.0 - Icon/Conf. | WrPa | Wrp1 |
| Retrospect 2.0 - Log | WrPa | TEXT |
| Retrospect 2.0 - Update from 1.3 | WrPa | WarD |
| SAT - Celina V1 | DSAT | SATT |
| SimAnt | SANT | SAGM |
| SimEarth | MYCR | SAVE |
| SimLife - Animals | SMLS | SPAL |
| SimLife - data | SMLS | SLZO |
| SimLife - Plants | SMLS | SPPL |
| SimLife - Zoo | SMLS | SLAS |
| Smart Alarms - Reminders | JOHN | RMDR |
| Smart Forms - Forms | KCFD | CFRM |
| Smartcom - data | SCOM | SCO1 |
| Smartcom - Help | SCOM | SCOO |
| Soft AT - data | PCXT | PCDT |
| Soft AT - Share PC | PCSH | APPL |
| Sound Edit Pro - Help | jBox | jBhp |
| Sound Edit Pro - Hyper Sound | STAX | WILD |
| Sound Edit Pro - Mac Recorder Driver | MRec | INIT |
| Sound Edit Pro - Music | jBox | jB1 |
| Sound Edit Pro - Preferences | jBox | jBpr |
| Sound Edit Pro - Serial Sw. | bpas | cdev |
| Sound Play - data | FSSC | FSSD |

| Program Name | Creator Code | File Type |
|---|---|---|
| Studio Session - Player | JAMS | APPL |
| Studio Session - Songs | XPRT | XSNG |
| StuffIt Deluxe - Installer | SIDN | APPL |
| StuffIt Deluxe - Scripts | SIT! | TEXT |
| StuffIt Deluxe - Stuffed Files | SIT! | SITD |
| StuffIt Deluxe 2.0 - Self Unstuffer | AUSt | SIT! |
| StuffIt Deluxe 2.0 - sit Converter | SITE | APPL |
| StuffIt Deluxe 2.0 - Unstuff | SDQK | SKex |
| StuffIt Deluxe 2.0 - Unstuff Deluxe | USTD | APPL |
| StuffIt Deluxe 3.0 - Unstuffit | Arfz | APPL |
| StuffIt Space Saver - MM Extension | MAGM | FEXT |
| StuffIt Space Saver - StuffIt Eng. | SITE | APPL |
| Suitcase 2.0 | S112 | Init |
| SuperCard - Bridge | BRID | APPL |
| SuperCard - Global Editors | RUNT | MDOC |
| SuperCard - Preferences | MANP | MPPF |
| SuperCard - Super Edit | MANP | APPL |
| SuperPaint - Doc | SPNT | SPTG |
| SuperPaint - Preferences | SPNT | SPPF |
| Swamp Gas - Color | SGas | CSGp |
| Swamp Gas - Color Map | SGas | CSwp |
| Swamp Gas - Configuration | SGas | CFig |
| Swamp Gas - Map USA | SGas | Swmp |
| Switcher - data | SWIT | SWIT |
| Swivel 3D - data | SWVL | SMDL |
| Talking Moose - Phrases | CdMn | MOOP |
| Talking Moose - Talking Finder | uins | uins |
| TeachText | ttxt | ttro |
| Tempo II Macros | TNP2 | TMP |
| Think C - data | KAHL | LSD |
| Think C - Debugger | KAHL | TEST |
| Think C - Project | KAHL | PROJ |
| Think Pascal - Interface Library | PJMM | OBT |
| Think Tank - data | TANK | TEXT |
| Thunderscan - data | SCAN | SCAN |
| TouchBase - data | GDEX | GDEX |
| TouchBase - Preferences | TBAS | PRES |
| TouchBase - Tools | TBUT | APPL |
| True Basic - Binder | TRU1 | APPL |
| True Basic - Program | TRUE | TEXT |
| Typestry - data | PXPM | PICT |
| TypeReader - data | TRUS | TRDa |
| TypeReader - Dictionary | TRUS | TDct |

| Program Name | Creator Code | File Type |
|---|---|---|
| TypeReader - Help | TRUS | TRHp |
| TypeReader - User Dictionary | TRUS | UDct |
| TypeStyler - AGFA Fonts | TSLR | TFNT |
| TypeStyler - Help | TSLR | THLP |
| TypeStyler - Samples | TSLR | TSDC |
| TypeStyler - Smooth Mover | SFMV | APPL |
| TypeStyler - Universal | TSLR | TSDC |
| Ultra Paint - Color Tables | ULTR | drwC |
| Ultra Paint - data | ULTR | UPNT |
| Ultra Paint - Help | ULTR | BIFF |
| Ultra Paint - Preferences | ULTR | UPRF |
| Ultra Paint - Tools | ULTR | TOOL |
| Uninvited - data | MCV2 | MCV2 |
| VersaTerm-PRO | SLip | APPL |
| VersaTerm-PRO - Command Set | VRRO | CMDS |
| VersaTerm-PRO - Control Slip | SLiP | cdev |
| VersaTerm-PRO - FP Server | TFFs | cdev |
| VersaTerm-PRO - FTM Tools | cnbf | fbnd |
| VersaTerm-PRO - Help | HEP2 | TEXT |
| Version Master - data | VMST | VMPF |
| Version Master - Preferences | VMST | VMPR |
| Version Master Data Base | VMST | VMDB |
| Vette - data | VETT | DATA |
| VideoShop - Changes | VShp | Vflt |
| VideoShop - Effects | VShp | Vxsn |
| VideoShop - Effects | VShp | Vxsx |
| VideoShop - Effects | VShp | Vflt |
| VideoShop - Hotel | TVOD | MooV |
| VideoShop - Visual Info. | hpsl | vigC |
| Video Works - data | MMVW | VWSC |
| Video Works - data | MMVW | DATA |
| Virtus' WalkThrough - data | VwlK | VMDL |
| Virtus' WalkThrough - Library | VwlK | VLIB |
| Vision Lab - Preferences | JRVL | Pref |
| Wealth Builder - Animations | MONY | Waim |
| White Knight - Filters | WK11 | RFLT |
| White Knight - Phone Book | WK11 | PBOK |
| White Knight - Proc. Edit | WK11 | PREP |
| White Knight - Procedure | WK11 | RRCP |
| White Knight - Stuff | WK11 | RES2 |
| Wingz - data | WNGZ | WZSS |
| Wingz - Help | WNGZ | WZHP |
| Wingz - Script | WNGZ | WZSC |

| Program Name | Creator Code | File Type |
|---|---|---|
| Word - File | WORD | PCOD |
| Word 4.0 - Conv Word Perf | PSPT | VISA |
| Word 4.0 - DATA | MSWD | WDBN |
| Word 4.0 - DCA to RFT/RTF | PSPT | visa |
| Word 4.0 - Dictionary | MSWD | DCT5 |
| Word 4.0 - Formula Set | MSWD | WSET |
| Word 4.0 - Glossary | MSWD | GLOS |
| Word 4.0 - Help | MSWD | WHLP |
| Word 4.0 - Hyphen | MSWD | WPRD |
| Word 4.0 - Macros | MCWA | MKDC |
| Word 4.0 - Thesaurus | WFO1 | THO2 |
| Word 5.0 - Grammar | WDSE | WDIC |
| Word 5.0 - Spelling | WDGE | WDIC |
| WordPerfect - Dictionary | SSIW | WPSP |
| WordPerfect - Dictionary, user | SSIW | WPDC |
| WordPerfect - Documents | SSIW | WPDO |
| WordPerfect - Thesaurus | SSIW | WPTH |
| WordPerfect Works - Database | BWks | BWdb |
| WordPerfect Works - Dictionary | WBks | UDCT |
| WordPerfect Works - Draw | BWks | BWdr |
| WordPerfect Works - Import Filters | WBks | Fltr |
| WordPerfect Works - Paint | BWks | BWpt |
| WordPerfect Works - Spreadsheet | BWks | BWss |
| WordPerfect Works - Thesaurus | WBks | WFDT |
| WordPerfect Works - USA Spelling | WBks | MDCT |
| WordPerfect Works - WP | BWks | BWwp |
| WriteNow - Dictionary | nX^n | nX^w |
| WriteNow - Doc | nX^n | nX^d |

# INDEX